Where are the Men in the House?

Discipling that Makes a Difference

By
Eric A. Johnson

Foreword by
Dr. A. Russell Awkard

Edited by
Claude R. Royston

Published by
BK Royston Publishing,
Jeffersonville, IN

BK Royston Publishing
P. O. Box 4321
Jeffersonville, IN 47131
502-802-5385
http://bkroystonpublishing.com

© Copyright 2013 – Eric A. Johnson

All Rights Reserved. No part of this book may be reproduced, stored in a retrieval system, or transmitted by any means without the written permission of the author.

Published by: BK Royston Publishing LLC
Cover Design by: Snorten Designs
Layout by: BK Royston Publishing LLC

ISBN-13: 978-0-9859439-3-6

Unless otherwise indicated, all scripture text is from the King James Version of the Bible.

Printed in the United States of America

ACKNOWLEDGEMENTS

This book has been my attempt to be "faithful over a few things." I am blessed to have had "a great cloud of witnesses" in my life, who have greatly encouraged me to press on.

I am blessed to have Ernestine Johnson as a mother who instilled in me early on that nothing beats determination, dedication, and duty.

The late Rev. J. R. Mitchell and Mrs. C. B. Mitchell have provided consistent encouragement to me and lived out before an inspiring example of faithful service and commitment to God's people.

Rev. and Mrs. C. F. Robertson and the New Mount Calvary Baptist Church, Terrell, Texas, Rev. and Mrs. F. J. H. Hobbs and the Mount Nebo Baptist Church, Victoria, Texas; and Rev. and Mrs. Walter Malone and the Canaan Baptist Church, Louisville, Kentucky are all owed a debt of gratitude for their patience, support and for providing me an opportunity to fulfill my vocation.

Danny Akin has helped me think through difficult issues with compassion and grace and chaired the committee which guided this thesis. T. Vaughn Walker has shown great confidence in my abilities and has graciously endured my evolving theological concepts about ministry. James Cox continues to remind me of the vital necessity of a strong pulpit ministry. F. Bruce Williams has shown himself to be a true friend. Robert Smith, Jr., a father and beloved friend, has inspired me to consider "the head and the heart."

A special and tender appreciation is due to my wife Jan, who has been faithful to "see it through" even when what we saw was struggle and sacrifice. To Erica, my daughter, and companion in silence and laughter.

        I am indebted to Mrs. Gladys A. Brent who has been a blessing in due season to me. Without her skills, this book would be lacking. I am appreciative to the Galilee Baptist Church staff and family, Louisville, Kentucky who has challenged me to be all that God would have me be and cared for me so that they could be all God called them to be.

                                        Eric A. Johnson

                                      Louisville, Kentucky

DEDICATION

To "the man of the house" who gave me my opportunity for life;

To my sons, J.R. and Wynton, whose living brings hope for our destiny;

To the men who are the Men of the House;

To our Christ who brings vision into existence!

                Ache Pa Ti,
                Dr. Eric A. Johnson

FOREWORD

How does it feel to read and book only to discover that you have been wrong for over 40 years? Ask me.

Dr. Eric Johnson's new book reveals a clear and well-researched message about the problems and possibilities with men in today's church. Drawing on the observations from ministerial leaders, past and present, he lays down the foundation stones for building strong Christian men. His academic research is backed up by the writer's practical experience in his pastorate.

Where are the men in the house? This piercing question tempts many pastors to be less than truthful. Like boasting about the size of church membership, and we have a tendency to blow-up the numbers of men who are active in the congregation. Dr. Johnson's book exposes a flaw in contemporary church life, regardless of public perceptions about size and success.

Shortly after preaching my first sermon in April 1966, I stopped by the home of a distant cousin. He happened to be my same age and was my best friend in high school. His father was a contemporary of my father. At that point, both of our dads were irregular in their attendance on Sundays. They were great fathers but not the kind of church members that pastors depend on. On my first visit to my cousin's house after becoming a 21-year-old minister, his father surprised with a piece of unsolicited advice. He said something like this, "Keep the men happy, because the women will always be happy to be in church."

Church leaders must become tuned in to the unique needs of men. Men don't have the same views about church that women seem to take for granted. The church must become more balanced in order to reach more men. Unfortunately, the nugget of truth that popped out of the mouth of my buddy's dad went largely unheeded for the next 40 years. What a pity!

Dr. Johnson's publication builds a sound argument for reshaping the way we "do" church. The ideas that he shares from his own pastoral achievements and from a rich variety of other sources are doable. We may not be able to change everything all at once, but it's time to make the church more welcoming, appealing and fulfilling to men.

Dr. A. Russell Awkard
Louisville, KY

TABLE OF CONTENTS

Chapter 1 INTRODUCTION — 1

   The Urgency and Mandate of Biblical Discipleship — 6

   African American Church Tradition. — 13

   Difficulties in Discipleship. — 26

Chapter 2 THE TWO GREAT INSTITUTIONS. — 50

   Family and Extended Family — 53

   Faith: Our Journey in the Church. — 73

   Challenges — 81

Chapter 3 MODELS OF MINISTRY — 106

   Ministry of Empowerment — 118

   Ministry of Resocialization — 125

   Ministry of Accountability — 132

   Ministry of Fellowship — 144

Chapter 4 CONCLUSION — 155

ENDNOTES — 160

BIBLIOGRAPHY — 189

CHAPTER 1

INTRODUCTION

The Christian Church in the twenty-first century and in a new millennium still faces many significant and difficult obstacles which challenge the teaching and practice of cruciform living. These challenges derive both from within and from without ranging from spiritual malfeasance grounded in a superficial worship which results in an entertainment theology,[1] to the loss of the "unique" distinctiveness of the Christ[2] as the Lord and Saviour of the world in a postmodern and pluralistic society.

The church faces an enormous task in attempting to be true to the biblical imperative of being salt, light, transformation and living sacrifices in a world saturated with cultural relativism and declining morality. Yet, the church faces worthy challenges from within the community of faith as well. Commitment and recruitment among church membership for volunteering in ministry competes with personal conveniences and believers whose schedules are too busy and complex to fulfill the great commission. Many congregations are simply satisfied to swap sheep and count numbers rather than evangelizing and discipling their communities and congregations.

As difficult as these challenges may appear, they are not new in their orientation; rather they have existed from the genesis of the church. One of the oldest challenges to mark the churches' second millennium is this challenge to make, mark and mature the disciples.[3] While we can clearly see the biblical (gospel) progression in making, marking, and maturing the disciples, one must note that a further biblical mandate is found in the Acts

> "One of the oldest challenges to mark the churches' second millennium is this challenge to make, mark and mature the disciples."

of the Apostles. This mandate is to multiply the disciples. John's gospel points in this direction in John 15:1-8 when we understand that the "fruit" Jesus speaks of in this text is people, but it is in Acts that one observes this principle clearly applied.

The evangelism and discipleship imperatives of the church are of even greater importance because of shifting morals and values, eroding culture, emphasis on materialism and less of a God-consciousness[4] in this post-traditional church, post-modern and pluralistic age.

There are at least twenty-nine references in the gospels to the word disciple (*mathetes*). There are 243 references in scripture to the disciples in general. In the Old Testament, the word disciple is found only once in Isaiah 8:16. Here the word is linked to the idea of being taught and learning (*limmud*). Each of these

> "A disciple is one who not only is a learner, follower, and student, but a professing practitioner.."

references articulates an understanding of a disciple as a learner, pupil or follower.[5] A disciple is one who is taught a set of principles or beliefs from a greater teacher. Usually in scripture this refers to Jesus' disciples, John's disciples or the general term disciples as a group of people.

The disciples' emphasis on learning is given in the derivation of the word. *Manthano* means "to learn," the Latin etymology of the word disciple translates to "a scholar." Here one notes not only the connotation of a pupil, learner and follower being taught a set of beliefs or principles, but also the foundation of the pupil practicing and adhering to the beliefs. A disciple is one who not only is a learner, follower, and student, but a professing practitioner. G. H. Trever quotes Forrar on the meaning of a disciple of Christ. "The disciple of Christ today may be described as one who believes His doctrines, rests upon His sacrifice, imbibes His spirit, and imitates His example."

This understanding and articulation of the

marriage of belief and behavior, principle and praxis is shown again in Trever's article when he gives the reader the etymology of *matheteuo*, a verb which indicates the literal passive--"was a disciple of Jesus" (Matt 27:57). In *Vine's Expository Dictionary* this relationship is again raised (Matt 13:52 "had been made a disciple").

This issue of evangelism and discipleship is even of greater importance to the African American community and church. Willie Richardson, in *Reclaiming the Urban Family: How to Mobilize the Church as a Family Training Center*, is correct when he asserts that the greatest challenge of the church today is to save families.[6] There are a multiplicity of critical issues in urban areas which affect the stability, spirituality and structure of urban families. The African American church as the major institution of influence and independency[7] is called upon to speak to these issues from both a Christ centered and community concerned position. This response has been grounded in what Henry and Ella Mitchell have termed "Black Spirituality" or "ole" Time Religion.[8] This spirituality[9] is grounded in another worldly identity which holds that one is possessed by the real presence of the Holy Spirit and infused in their actions to live out daily this possession, being made into the image of Christ and following all Christ would have them do.[10] Western theology terms this "incarnational discipleship."

The Urgency and Mandate of Biblical Discipleship

> "...evangelistic, discipleship oriented and Christ centered response to the spiritual void and social ills of the city.."

There is an urgent need in the urban areas of America (particularly in the African American communities) for an evangelistic, discipleship oriented and Christ centered response to the spiritual void and social ills of the city (particularly in the area of family nurture). Daryl Ward has listed at least four main "Gaps."[11] Ward notes in his article that cities are comprised of all types of persons and perspectives, but this does not preclude "Gaps." Ward articulates at least four "GAP" areas: economic, employment, educational, and ethnic gaps.[12] Ward suggests that "Gaps" are not places utilized for permanent dwelling. They are not meant for positive dwelling, rather Ward asserts that "Gaps" derive from structures which failed to hold together under some form of pressure that shook, pulled, or pressed until it cracked.[13]

Ward posits his thought in Ezekiel 22:29-30.

> The people of the land have used oppression, and exercised robbery, and have vexed the poor and needy: yea, they have oppressed the stranger wrongfully. And I sought for a man among them that should make up the hedge, and stand in the gap before me for the land, that I should not destroy it: but I found none.

The first gap discussed by Ward is the economic gap. He shares with the reader that in the United States the top 1 percent of citizens now earns more of the nation's wealth than the bottom 40 percent.[14] This makes the United States the most economically unequal country in the industrialized world.

Economics is an important factor to be addressed

in the church's attempt to make the lives of persons more livable, to gain a hearing for the gospel, and disciple African American men. This issue has been addressed in the African American community by returning to the self-determination ethic of the Reconstruction Era Black Church. During Reconstruction, Black pastors and their congregations began burial societies (insurance companies), funeral homes, schools, and banks to create jobs and industry for persons newly freed from slavery without a stable and steady income. Today this approach has refined its methodology.[15] Many urban churches have established Federal Credit Unions, non-profit development corporations, and have incorporated themselves to ensure an ecclesiastical response to redress the economic depravity common among inner city dwellers. As the tax base and infrastructure of the inner city declines, jobs move out to other areas and the church has to respond to restore some stability and opportunities for an oppressed people.[16]

The second gap discussed by Ward was employment. It has already been noted that there is strong correlation between the lack of adequate and just employment and high crime rates. This can be seen throughout all urban areas. Particularly this is crucial for young African American male youth. Inner city Black youth have an unemployment rate over twice that of white youth.[17] This emphasis on the employment of African American men is not normally discussed under the theme of discipleship, however, employment should be included because the rite of passage called "doing time" must be stopped in African American youth (male) and community.[18]

> "Educational emphasis must also be included in our discipleship model"

Educational emphasis must also be included in our discipleship model. This is because 82 percent of youth in jail are high school dropouts.[19] Tragically, building state-of-the-art prisons[20] have become a million-dollar industry while many inner city (public education) schools are either falling apart or closing.

Education must not be limited to three R's, rather Christian education must be stressed. What seems to be helpful are ministries such as Rites of Passage or camps that stress a holistic approach to excellence in education. These "cultural" ministries are similar to Boy Scouts or Girl Scouts, but have a strong "discipline" component.[21]

A final gap investigated was the ethnic gap. Ward argues that half of the American workforce will soon be women and minorities. These are persons who are often at a disadvantage.[22] The church of Jesus Christ has to consider this fact when seeking to disciple persons in the community, and it must find methods to assist persons who may struggle because of ethnic issues.

What kind of church, evangelism or discipleship ministry will be able to make a difference in this type of complex social matrix? Ward lifts two pragmatic paradigms of ministry to answer this dilemma. In realizing the historical importance of the African American church, and that if these issues are to be resolved in a method which lifts Jesus (John 12:32), Ward, therefore, argues that there exists two possible paradigms of church ministry.

> "Transitional churches are pointed inward."

The first paradigm of church ministry he calls transitional churches.[23] Normally, transitional churches are thought to be white and older, located geographically in neighborhoods which are transitioning economically and racially. However, there are African American churches which also fit this category. These are churches (predominately African American) which have not stayed on the cutting edge or even kept abreast of the changes in cultural and society. These churches are locked into one certain paradigm of what ministry is and one method of theological praxis.

Transitional churches are pointed inward.[24] These churches are pointed inward in their mindset and do not see themselves as needing to change their focus. These churches are dependent upon their past

> "Transformative churches.. develop methods of evangelism and discipleship that assist the church in developing the desire and discipline to carry out the 'Great Commission'.."

exploits and heritage. This makes their main ministry a ministry of maintenance and inward focus.[25] Because their focus is not outward or upward, there is no need for ingenuity to "go out and make disciples." There is no need to go into the neighborhood and be witnesses because the priority rests with maintaining the status quo.

The second ministry paradigm is the transformative church.[26] This church is rooted in Paul's New Testament idea that the basic essence of a believer is transformation.[27] Paul and Ward argue for an internal change resulting in an external transformation of creation. Transformative churches are those churches which pursue and continue to develop methods of evangelism and discipleship that assist the church in developing the desire and discipline to carry out the "Great Commission" in revolutionary methods. Ward utilizes the four point method of Rosabeth Moss Kanter to empower members to get involved in bringing about transformational discipleship:

1. Give people important work to do on critical issues,
2. Give people discretion and autonomy over their tasks and resources,
3. Give visibility to others and provide recognition for their efforts,

4. Building relationships for others connecting them with powerful people and finding them sponsors and mentors.[28]

This empowerment methodology can be used to build, develop and strengthen discipleship ministries in our churches.

The African American Church Tradition

There exists very little written material from "the invisible institution"[29] on discipleship or evangelism. This lack of discipleship or evangelism curriculum is in no way to suggest that the act of disciple making and evangelism were lost or absent.

Because of the historical holocaust and atrocities which were perpetuated upon persons of African descent,[30] the ministry which derives from the African experience and church is not a written word, but rather exists as an oral and coded language, heritage and pragmatic methodology. African culture is rooted in an oral culture and all important things were transmitted through the oral tradition as opposed to the written word.[31] This is a unique method of discipleship.

This model of faith transference is also seen with

Paul and his young companions Timothy and Titus in 1 Timothy 3:18-20; 4:13-15; 2 Timothy 2:1-3; 2:14-19; 3:14-15; Titus 2:1-10; 3:8-11. African culture has this one component of oral transference in common with Hebraic culture. In Deuteronomy 6, the Shema is a spoken oral tradition from the father to his son. Also Jesus was a recipient of the oral traditions passed down to him and he utilized the oral tradition in teaching his disciples.

Much of the discipleship in the African American community has occurred through the oral tradition. It is not uncommon in the African American church to see young men being instructed in righteousness by older men and older women sharing with younger women. This is particularly true as it relates to older more experienced pastors instructing younger ministers (pastors) and church officers such as deacons, trustees and various laity ministries instructing those coming on behind them. This is also true for ministers' wives, deaconesses (deacon's wives) and other laity led ministry positions. The discipleship or mentoring relationship has been present although narrow and not systematically structured. When looking for discipleship resources for the needs of African American congregations, the resources are greatly limited. When farther narrowed to meet the needs of urban African American men, the resources are almost non-existent.[32]

When considering the evangelization and discipleship of African American men, one must take into consideration the strong oral tradition of African American culture, the informal means and methodology of discipleship of African American churches, the lack of or unimportance of systematized and organized structure by which to disciple/evangelize and the communal aspect represented in the strong person to person relations emphasized in the African American church. This model represents not an individualistic understanding of discipleship, but rather a communal effort through personal relationships. This is not to say that the African American church is deficient, but it operates in a different church tradition and perspective.

The major form of evangelism and discipleship in the majority of African American churches is pastoral preaching and teaching, and the major discipler is the pastor. As a worship driven organism, the majority of the transformation, conviction and challenge are lodged in the preaching and Sunday worship experience. This again is a cultural idiom.[33] When the pastor speaks or teaches, the congregation is more sensitive to receive his word because he is the "incarnational shepherd"--and they are under his leading.

> "The major form of evangelism and discipleship... is pastoral preaching and teaching."

In African thought, the pastor is the chief, the priest-king and unifier of all different tribes and languages. Although his functions were not perceived as Christian by his masters, he became what was necessary to meet the need of his people.

> One errs in assuming that the slave preacher was not primarily Christian and did not play a variety of roles, especially that of African priest. Indeed, the categories of religious leadership on plantations were often indistinguishable, as they were in cities. The preacher's priestly or African function, and that of deacon, and class leader, was guarded from whites, who thought anything African of a religious nature was pagan or heathen, an insult to Christianity. Therefore, if the African religious leader was to

> operate in the open, the safest cloak to hide behind was that of Christianity. African religious leaders predominated in slavery and in that oppressive environment orchestrated their people's transformation into a single people culturally. James Weldon Johnson makes the penetrating observation that it was through the Negro preachers that "people of diverse languages and customs who were brought here from diverse parts of Africa and thrown into slavery were given their first sense of unity and solidarity."[34]

This quotation gives one insight into the cultural matrix that the African American pastor is still considered the "chief" evangelist and discipler.[35] Although slavery and oppression removed from the African some of his Africanisms, slavery failed to break the attachment between the priest-king and his people, pastor and sheep, and father to his children.[36] Here one must be aware that this relationship is earned, no hireling can come in the congregation and expect to immediately become the role model and prime example of behavior and influence for his congregation.

One of the developments to evolve from the barbarian treatment of the captive Africans during the holocaust of American slavery was the "Black Church". With the development of the Black church comes the reconfiguration of the African chief into the Black Church pastor or the slave preacher. The slave preacher's role was often no more than that of an "exhorter."[37] This role ranged from being allowed to "exercise his gift" to being supervised by a white preacher and either being called on to give after thoughts to the sermon or get the congregation prepared for the "main" sermon.[38]

    Another role which gives credence to the importance of the pastor as the major influence on his congregation as it relates to discipleship is that preaching is the center of worship in African American churches. As the center of worship, the preacher and his preaching by speech and example set the tone for what will be learned and applied in the congregation's Christian daily life. This portrait is valid for several historical reasons. First, the slave "exhorter" gave the captives optimism in the midst of a dark circumstance. He reminded them that no matter how difficult and bleak the situation, God's power to deliver them was not limited. The liberation motif found in Exodus 13 and 14 and other passages provided the foundation for his belief in the face of hopelessness. The slave preacher utilized spiritual creativity in preaching his message of deliverance and redemption. Through his preaching, the captives received help, hope and healing.[39] They received the necessary hope and strength to endure their trials. This strengthening came through both the corporate worship and the preaching event. This is an obvious point considering that in many instances both the slaves and their preacher risked their lives to gather together for the opportunity to worship and celebrate. Worship was the key to their survival[40] and worship can play an integral role in reclaiming men for the kingdom of God. The jubilant and emotional celebration found in the worship experience resulted from the creativity utilized by the slave exhorters who spoke the word so vividly that despite the misery of slavery, joy and enthusiasm were present in their lives.

Another important historical factor which makes the African American pastor a strong influence or discipler is the fact that during slavery, the slaves were not allowed to congregate or communicate in crowds, so the slave exhorter was responsible for devising a way of ministering to the slaves.[41] It was out of the need to communicate about worship that the coded language of the spirituals grew. The slaves would sing and the preacher would preach in code. Again, one notes that the historical unity of the captives, the invisible institution[42] and slave religion[43] were all in part a result of the efforts of the slave exhorter. It is for this reason that black preaching and pastoring should not be considered outside the accepted and "orthodox" mainstream of where God is at work in the world.[44]

This culture phenomenon has helped not only the slaves, but also today's Black church experience. This point can be seen even in the twenty-first century. The Black preacher has always held certain fundamental concrete and nonnegotiable tenets regarding faith and practice and as a result of this, one can observe these same strong and tenacious tenets in most if not all African American congregations to this present day. In particular, the preacher was accustomed to great amounts of memorized material. The African priest/pastor was required as a leader to memorize all heritage and proverbs, so that when called upon he would be able to utilize the necessary truth or wisdom needed for that specific situation.[45] The Bible was learned much in the same way through oral transmission and memorization. Even today in the African American church, congregations believe it to be a "special gift" to preach without the utilization of paper and many preachers strive to preach without notes. This preaching is not necessarily extemporaneous, but rather a message well prepared and memorized. This tradition reflects itself in several ways. The importance of scripture memorization shows that African Americans want to be a people of the word. To be a serious African American Christian or preacher you must be known for knowing (memorizing) the word. Second, is the place of priority given to scripture. Because it was important historically, it finds a prominent place in the worship life of the church and the believer.[46] As it relates to discipleship, this emphasis on the supremacy, priority and memorization of the word which was transferred from the slave preacher to the slaves is crucial in making disciples who are influenced by the word of God. Mitchell is correct when he asserts that:

> what blacks have done with the Bible has been to keep all of the strengths of the so-called primitive approach in the Bible, while at the same time absorbing and integrating the intellectual world view we now have, without letting it kill the religion . . . there is nowhere near the same kind of approach to the Bible. The result has been that the average black audience would not listen to a preacher for five minutes if he didn't have a text. This is a tremendous strength. The kinds of doctrinal positions that the Bible suggests, again, have been taken very seriously; but not with the rigidity that makes people go to such extremes like they call them in the intellectual world, reductio ad absurdum.[47]

Discipleship as represented in the slave preacher was word based, but it was also concerned with contemporary experience and relevance.[48] Craig Loscalzo, in his volume, *Preaching Sermons that Connect*, utilizes the model of Kenneth Burke to argue that our ministry of preaching ought to register, reach, or find one's audience in the pew. Loscalzo calls this effective communication through identification.[49] The slaves upon hearing the black preacher quickly understood and were fully aware that he was a Bible-centered preacher, but also a very life-oriented preacher.[50] Just as the slave exhorter spoke to the life issues of his time, we are also to speak to those same life issues of today. Discipleship must answer the question of praxis in daily living. This answer was provided by the black pulpit each time the slaves assembled for "secret worship." The slave preacher spoke to both existential and eternal concerns.

> Since the first Africans set foot on this soil, people of African descent have had a singularly unique experience in the new world. They brought with them an inherent philosophical heritage, including a distinctive religious sensibility; they encountered the most brutal forms of slavery in human history; and they were introduced to North Atlantic Christianity. Because there was no precedent for the experience of people of African descent, they created distinctive ways of conceptualizing and speaking about their ultimate concerns.[51]

Another discipleship aspect is noted in the understanding that the Black church was born out of slavery.[52] As such, the preaching arose from a hopeful attempt to give life to those on the margins of existence struggling to survive despite little tangible evidence that surviving was a legitimate option. Yet, the preaching of this era prized freedom and pushed for dignity, self-worth and a mentality of protest and resistance.[53] Freedom and spirituality were to be prized and regarded as necessities for the "pilgrim's journey" and even some 300 years later, freedom is still important in African American churches. Discipleship, should inculcate an understanding of freedom translated from sound scriptural basis.

Freedom as a theme within discipleship should maintain an ontology of integrity, yet affirm the privilege of allowing God to work through the authentic self. This principle is clearly seen in Black preaching. While preaching a minister may jump, remove his coat or tie, raise his hands, run down the aisles or give some unusual form of gesticulation. Despite these happenings, the African American congregations know that if the preacher is sincere, it is simply the freedom of the preacher and congregation to allow the preacher to be used by God in a manner that is authentic to the vessel. This translates into a discipleship principle in that as the preacher preaches pragmatically, he is showing the congregation that to be a

> "Discipleship, should inculcate an understanding of freedom translated from sound scriptural basis."

disciple is to give one's self completely in surrender to the service of the Master.[54]

The final distinctive of the Black preacher's discipleship of his congregation is rooted in the previous item discussed. For wherever there is the Spirit of the Lord, there is liberty[55] and this liberty brings to the captives a reason to celebrate. Celebration has long been the hallmark of African Traditional Religion (ATR). Even prior to the slavery enterprise, traditional African worship required celebration.[56] King notes that the celebration was unrehearsed and undirected. It was a joyful enthusiasm which amazes other persons looking from the outside in.[57] The source of the slave's joy was that they knew God would deliver, and they trusted in God's providence and sovereignty. King further states that this celebration was also a time to renew their commitment to God and renew their pledge in gratitude for all God had done and would do for them.[58]

Celebration as a discipleship tenet should reflect the joy that can be articulated and expressed from serving the Lord. The disciples or believers realize that despite difficulties, the Lord will provide.[59] Celebration also includes the awareness that unlike the slaves, one can come into an open door no man can shut; second, that in celebration one gives thanks not only for those gifts previously given, but also for those yet to be received; it is to celebrate the things hoped for, the evidence of things unseen (Hebrews 11:1).[60] This celebration for the slave preacher and congregation centered in the person of Christ, the one who has all power, the Alpha and Omega, the way, truth and the life. Like the early African

> "Celebration as a discipleship tenet should reflect the joy...from serving the Lord."

captives, one must celebrate in the centrality of Christ even in the midst of vicious atrocities.[61]

Difficulties in Discipleship

Evangelism and discipleship ministries face a difficult and uphill battle in this postmodern and pluralistic society. If this presupposition is true among the dominant cultural milieu, how much more serious is this challenge among alienated, urban dwelling poor, under-educated, unemployed, and the disenfranchised. For the urban masses of men who are often times (in my congregation) forced to work on Sunday because they need to provide on Monday, the priority of work and survival (sustenance) takes precedence over church attendance. This dilemma is one of the many difficulties one will face in attempting to disciple men.

The first difficulty that should be addressed is whether or not the men who are being discipled have genuinely committed themselves to a saving personal relationship to Jesus as their Lord and Saviour. This is a crucial aspect not only in one's methodology, but also for the genesis of living a transformed life. Romans 10:9-12:1, 2; John 3:3-7; 16, 17; Acts 4:12; and 2 Corinthians 5:17 are all periscopes which present a clear understanding of the necessity of Jesus as the major component for a transformed life. The challenge here is twofold. In an effort to maintain numbers or appear to be fulfilling the Great Commission, many churches have lowered the requirements to a "pseudo" discipleship; they may emphasize areas such as financial support, consistent attendance, family ties or the ability to influence people over the salvation mandate.[62] Thus, churches may be guilty of attempting to disciple men not yet won to the Lord.

The second aspect relates to an unclear defining or inability to delineate the gospel in concrete terms, thereby illuminating what a disciple of Jesus Christ is and what this change means as it relates to personal cost and sacrifice.[63] Men who are committed to Jesus may not understand the process of discipleship because it is not emphasized as a lifestyle for every believer regardless of position or place.

Jawanza Kunjufu, in his volume entitled *Adam, Where Are You? Why Most Black Men Don't Go to Church* shares twenty-one reasons for the difficulty found in discipling African American males or the lack of their presence in African American congregations.[64]

The first reason given was the hypocrisy in the church. Men believed that there was too much contradiction between what was being said and what was being done in the community. Second, men noted the difficulty they had in controlling their ego when it came to the pastor. Men desired to be in the leadership position and many times wish to have the "perceived" power of the pastor. Third, men had a difficult time continuing to believe in God or have faith in God during difficult circumstances such as the loss of a job or the death of a relative. Also, men stated that they had difficulty believing and accepting the forgiveness of God for their shortcomings.

Fourth, men shared their reluctance to be passive and turn the other cheek. They perceive that the injunction to turn the other cheek renders them passive toward others and toward social injustices. Application seems to be hindrances men have the hardest struggle with when looking at becoming more like Jesus.

> "..men stated that they had difficulty believing and accepting the forgiveness of God for their shortcomings."

Tithing was the fifth issue discussed as a barrier to discipleship and attendance in corporate worship. Giving is seen as not achieving a clear purpose. Men want to know where the money is going and what it is doing. Most men interviewed by Kunjufu felt that ten percent of one's income was too much to give the church. Another related issue was the erroneous assumption that most of the money was being given to the pastor while the church is not creating jobs or better opportunities for the community.

The sixth difficulty was the irrelevance of the traditional church. Men felt that the church did not address their problems. They failed to see how the King James Version of the Bible provided solutions for the problem of drugs, crime, teen pregnancy, unemployment, or recreational opportunities.

The seventh concern was the Eurocentric depiction of Jesus and other cultural persons. The question why or how Jesus got blonde hair and blue eyes (for men) relates to the self-hatred given to African Americans during slavery. Images and art play a major role in educating and strengthening men and they shared with Kunjufu the negative effect of not having a Jesus who can relate to you in your times of struggle and sadness.

The length of the worship experience was the eighth difficulty mentioned by the men. It was noted that Catholics complete mass in forty-five minutes, but other churches held up to three hours. The difficulty seems to be not so much the length, but the unorganized and loose way worship precedes in many churches.

The next difficulty was that the African American churches are too emotional in their worship experience. Some men felt as though all the shouting, dancing, hollering and stomping was not needed nor appreciated. Yet, the men noted the conflict of desiring to attend church and sports (time conflict). The men felt that churches could adapt their schedules around some of the major sports events.

The three difficulties[65] noted by Kunjufu were education, the lack of a Christian role model and the distinction between being spiritual and being religious. The ability of African American men to read has long hindered their participation and involvement in worship and in ministry. African American men find it difficult to understand what is being said by the pastor with his doctorate. How can they participate in the

> "African American men believe in God, but some do not know what to call Him."

responsive reading if one cannot read? Helping African American men with little education to feel a part of the church is crucial to a discipleship ministry.

Another significant area mentioned in Kunjufu's research was the lack of a Christian role model for African American men. Few of the African American men interviewed had someone they considered close to them to be a positive male Christ role model. The question African American men raised was--can one be anything that one has not seen? If one has never seen a saved African American man, can one truly become one? This question asserts the power of Jesus' challenge to the disciples in Matthew 5:13-16 to be (among others) as salt and light; to let our light shine so that others can see and glorify your Father which is in heaven.[66]

Syncretism and universalism have found their way into the lives of African American men as it relates to defining themselves as spiritual or being religious. African American men believe in God, but some do not know what to call Him.[67] The research reported that African American men feel that they are spiritual and good persons, but do not see the need to pay a ten percent admission fee to enter a building, see a male pastor, and to come to church.[68] Other men reported that their problem was with the belief that a certain religion was right and all others wrong and if one did not hold a certain view then they would be lost forever. Their point is that there are good ideas and principles in all religions, and they are going to continue studying all of them and reap all their benefits.[69] However, Acts 4:12 states that there is no other name under heaven given among men, whereby we must be saved, save the name of Jesus.[70]

William Harris' article "Why Most Black Men Won't Go to Church"[71] affirms the research of Kunjufu. Harris' article lifts seven reasons African American men are not in church. Harris suggests that this problem is not exclusively a cultural incident, rather most churches of all cultures and denominations lack men.

First, Harris suggests the African American men find the church hypocritical and untenable. For those men who are not employed or underemployed, it is difficult to sit through a worship experience with persons who are more concerned about their attire than the main reason they are there. Second, African American men resist churches because the church has not sought to accommodate men. Most church worship experiences are rigid and compete with various sporting events such as the National Football League or National Basketball Association. Therefore, men who want to spend their afternoons with their families feel they are in bondage if they attend church because of the length of time most African American churches utilize to worship.

Another difficulty in bringing men into the African American church is that the prevailing doctrine of today's Christian churches is illogical to the twentieth century man's mind. Here men are suggesting that loving one's enemies, blessing those who persecute one, and turning the other cheek are doctrines which many African American men find repulsive. The character and manhood of Jesus is also questionable as it relates to the effeminate way Jesus is presented.

The fourth reason men neglect the church is that the church is based on a love ethic in which the Heavenly is symbolized in earthly relationships. This is very difficult for African American men to understand considering that in order to understand a "Heavenly" father one looks at the earthly father and for many African American men there was no earthly father. The ideas of unconditional giving, nurture, protection, blessing, and total availability are far from clear.

> "an African American man.. will not draw near to a God that requires submission for an authentic relationship."

Fifth, African American males have a problem with submission to spiritual authority. Harris suggests that because of the oppressive structure of our society and the injustice faced by African American men, it is difficult for African American men to place themselves in what they may misunderstand as an inferior role. Submission to authority is not understood because there is no positive, consistent and relevant male model in the home. The result is an African American man that cannot or will not draw near to a God that requires submission for an authentic relationship.

African American men resist the church and being discipled because they have problems interpreting or understanding the preacher. The relationships between the pastor and men in the African American church have been strained because some men have felt they were forced into an inferior status all week and will not seek out another situation where they will be made to feel inferior. Unfortunately, this is why many African American men resist the church. The pastor is often built up by the women as charismatic and authoritative. When men do attend the worship experiences, Harris notes they are often greeted with sermons pointing out the failures of the men.

The final reason African American men resist the church is because the church seemingly does not address their needs. The church is seen as irrelevant to the issues of men in this society. Economic empowerment, job skills training, cooperative and creative economics and better advancement opportunities should be the order of the day. Yet, in many congregations these issues are not on the agenda.

F. Bruce Williams, pastor of the Bates Memorial Baptist Church, in a lecture on the new "endangered species"[72] addressed the difficulties of discipling African American men from a socio-religious perspective.[73] In this lecture, Williams notes that the church must address the reason that more African American men are in the criminal justice system than the educational system. The relevant question for the church or ministry which seeks to disciple African American men is in what way does our theology (discipleship) speak to the modern holocaust of the African American men's souls?

Williams sees five areas that must guide churches seeking to disciple men. First, because of the mis-education many men have received, they have a mistaken identity.[74] As a result of mis-education, African American men have been forced or conditioned to accept the identity others have given them and are not self-defined or Christ-defined. John 15:1-8 gives the model for one's connectedness and identity to Christ. This is not the way many African American men define themselves and therefore in their relationships with women they choose the hierarchical mentality of "I'm in charge," but in actuality this is not the case.

Second, African American men suffer from, misplaced priorities. As a result of decades of abject poverty and suffering, African American men believe it is more important to look good than live good. The definition and origin of respect (among African American men is derived from where one lives, not how one lives).[75]

Third, Williams posits that as a result of the mis-education and misplaced priorities, African American men are victimized by misguided spirituality. The popular perception of Jesus as blue eyed, effeminate, blond hair, and irrelevant to the contemporary issues of the African American community and men spills over into ecclesiology. Some churches are all worship and not involved in the community, while others are involved to the extent that worship suffers. What is needed is a holistic and balanced understanding of the church, her mission and mandate.

> "...men want a God they can manipulate for their own gain, pleasure and time."

Fourth, African American men suffer from a manipulative spirituality. Williams feels that African American men want a God they can manipulate for their own gain, pleasure and time. Yet, this mindset is not consistent with biblical revelation. God is sovereign in His rule and is righteous in all His acts.

The final aspect noted by Williams is the lack of celebration among men in worship. Williams suggests that many churches are not comfortable enough for men to really express themselves freely and yet Williams declares that men must decide to praise and feel comfortable whenever God is being praised.

William provides six solutions as a way of drawing African American men to church and ministry:

1. Tell men the benefits of salvation.
2. Encourage other men to be seen doing ministry.
3. Aggressive not passive evangelism.
4. Men must witness by example.
5. Present a correct Christ picture (not effeminate).
6. Teach men about their heritage and deal with the contemporary issues from a biblical and spiritual

perspective.[76]

Bill Hull, in *Disciple Making Pastor: The Key to Building Healthy Christians in Today's Church*, provides the rationale for why discipleship must again reclaim the heart of the churches mandate. Hull suggests that the organized church today has lost momentum and lost direction.[77] The modern evangelical church is confusing programming and membership promotions with fulfilling the Great Commission.[78]

> "The church must regain the integrity of making disciples that are healthy and which multiply."

Hull asserts correctly that the crisis at the heart of the church is a crisis of product.[79] African American men in three different studies have said that because they have difficulty seeing a Christian disciple, they have difficulty becoming a Christian disciple. John 15:7-17 describes Jesus' definition of a disciple as one who abides in Him, is obedient, bears fruit, glorifies God, has joy, and loves.[80] The church must regain the integrity of making disciples that are healthy and which multiply.

Like Hull, I am asserting that the evangelical

church is weak, self-indulgent and superficial[81] and that postmodern culture has "conformed the church" into its mold. This weakness of the church is noted by the idea that most congregations grow based on transference, not multiplication and few Christians are penetrating the world or trained to witness. Hull helps at this point when he argues not only are Christians untrained to penetrate their spheres of influence, their values have slipped as well.[82] Christians' use of money, priorities, time, and attitudes about work and leisure, divorce and remarriage, increasingly reflect culture rather than scripture. Therefore, the church is weak both in skills and in character.[83]

    Hull gives two strong reasons to place disciple making at the heart of the church. First, the need is seen in the condition of the church; its weakness is a mandate for corrective action. Second, pastors desire to place disciple making at the heart of the local church, but need a means and a model.[84]

    As a result of the weak conditions of our churches, there are some other difficulties to be noted:

1. methodological and resource issues for curriculum which speak to the urban the context.
2. misconceptions and poor definitions of what discipleship really is all about.[85]
3. methods of building and bridging relationships with those to be discipled (men).
4. encouraging men to come out to the physical facility and become involved.
5. showing the relevance of discipleship to contemporary issues.
6. weak leadership.[86]
7. reorientation for the church to disciple making and the urgency of this process.[87]
8. helping the church grasp the relationship between evangelism and discipleship.
9. eradicating mis-education among men about the role and historicity of the African American church and her Christ.

Thesis for Study

The discipleship of African American men must become an intentional, aggressive, and consistent focus and enterprise of the church. As such, the theology which undergirds this mandate and commission[88] must be grounded in biblical foundations and a pragmatic or action praxis. This

> "..discipleship of African American men must become an intentional, aggressive, and consistent focus and enterprise of the church."

theological praxis is oriented in the Christian understanding of transformation (2 Corinthians 5:17).

Evangelism is seen to be a method of bringing African American men (and persons) into a saving personal relationship with Jesus, which impacts and relates not only to the saving of their souls, but also provides them with a holistic perspective of salvation. This holistic perspective transforms every area of their life. African American men are then brought into a family where spiritual maturation occurs through discipleship and they are provided a positive and encouraging environment in which to discover God's purpose and mission for their lives. They are able to influence their families, communities, grapple with the difficult issues in their communities, and find Christ centered solutions for these areas which have previously kept African American men out of the church.

The intentional discipleship emphasis of the church should not only be an action praxis, but it should also appreciate and utilize the oral culture already present in the African American church. The church must develop and utilize curriculum which speaks to the importance and necessity of spiritual transformation,[89] faith development,[90] the perseverance or endurance of the saints[91] and the equipping of the saints with Christian principles to do ministry in their sphere of influence.[92] African American men will be equipped through discipleship to give an apologia[93] (defense) for the internal transformation within and the good works without.[94]

Intentional discipleship also must examine the kinds of art, artwork and literature that are utilized in teaching both young African American boys and men.[95] African American men have long seen the dichotomy between what the Bible says and what is often pictured or written about African American men. Some of the art and literature issues are those of context and culture, but others are issues of self-worth assassination.[96] Too often African

45

American men have been mislabeled, called culturally deprived, labeled to lack the equal academic ability of their white counter parts, and labeled to be nothing more than a domesticated beast.[97] However, the scriptures teach that all persons were created in the image of God.[98] Therefore, art, literature and Christian education and discipleship curriculum must do its part in presenting the un-fragmented truth about African American men, and teaching them that self-worth originates primarily in the Creator and His image in them.[99]

The discipleship emphasis is situated within the context of the church as family. Discipleship should take place within relationship. This relationship is best seen in the extended family understanding of the church which affords the church an opportunity to build a bridge to reach or "adopt" those outside the family. This "bridge" is multigenerational in its make-up and seeks to provide a mutual support system for

> "Discipleship should take place within relationship."

all those who may enter into the family.[100] This extended family exhibits at least three strengths according to Hannah. First, it is necessarily elastic. This is to say that the relational family must be able to expand in order to accommodate additional members.[101] Second, is the sense of oneness that exists between family members; a relationship of "interconnectedness." The extended family helps to shape and define the member's identity and values. Both accomplishments and acquired possessions are shared among the members of the extended family.[102] The last characteristic noted is the egalitarian view of sex roles. Each church member, whether male or female, is expected to fulfill complementary and interchangeable roles for the functioning of the unit and the strength of the network.[103]

This understanding of family provides the family of faith the opportunity to care for and minister to African American men who need assistance with issues in their life or families.

> "...intentional discipleship theology is that one looks for tangible and measurable outcomes..."

The second attribute of this family of God is that

it provides the spiritual food and environment for faith development as well as small focus groups on community issues that affect the lives of men within the community and church. This opportunity provides the men with a chance to find solutions and be active in making a significant difference.[104] Fourth, within the family of grace, African American men will be equipped for holistic Christian service and able to transmit "the faith once delivered to the saints unto others who may be under their influence.

The outcome of this type of intentional discipleship theology is that one looks for tangible and measurable outcomes which rest in a purpose and mission oriented ecclesiology as opposed to an event oriented ecclesiology. Through familial and spiritual kinship, persons are nurtured into a saving and loving relationship with Jesus and become empowered through Christian re-socialization and transformation to be accountable, responsible, and participate in the fellowship of the saints.

Research Methodology

Because this paper is addressing theology and discipleship models in the African American church, it will begin with a focus on the biblical mandate to make, mark, and mature male disciples, and then move to articulate the problems encountered by the church in the discipleship of men. Here the paper will also address the pastor's role in the discipleship of men. Also an examination of the role of the family as it relates to Black male discipleship will be investigated. Further, this paper will examine various discipleship models and the theology undergirding them in an attempt to provide a more effective discipleship model.

The resources utilized will include extensive interviews with several pastors who presently have effective ministry models for the discipleship of men. Second, journal articles and other volumes addressing the issues and problems of discipleship as it relates to men will be investigated. Third, a brief survey of Black family materials will be used to show various statistics about the Black family. Finally, videos and cassette tapes will be examined to document how discipleship and the African American male crisis are examined through preaching.

CHAPTER 2

THE TWO GREAT INSTITUTIONS

Within the African American community, there are two great institutions: the family and/or extended family and the church (the family of God). The vast importance and essential value of each of these institutions has been clearly proven to African Americans over time and through all the turbulent testing of history. Yet, contemporary times have presented new tribulations. What can be done to bring African American men into the Christian Church? Willie Richardson, in *Reclaiming The Urban Family*, suggests that the solution is saving families.

> The great challenge of the church today is to save families. In some cases, although we have been effective in the soul-saving of families, the families were destroyed because they did not know how to be a Christian family...we have to lead our churches and mobilize our congregations to get involved in saving and building families.[105]

Despite the middle passage, chattel slavery,

social mis-education,[106] psychological abuse, physical torment and emotional distress the African American family has been a viable means of help, hope and healing.[107] The family paradigm can also be a strong model for intentional evangelism and discipleship of African American men. This fact must not be ignored because of the innate importance of family and familial dynamics upon the lives of African American men.[108]

Of course, the importance of family is seen throughout Holy Scripture. From Genesis to Revelation, one notes the importance and particular order God gives to the family. Adam and Eve are created in the image of God and given dominion in the Garden of Eden (Gen 1:26-28, 2:15; 21-25) and from these two persons come all other families of the earth. Abram is chosen by God as the forefather to the nation (family) of Israel (Gen 12). God makes a covenant with this patriarch who prior to this theophany is unable (along with his wife) to have children (Gen 12). An important part

> "The family paradigm can also be a strong model for intentional evangelism and discipleship..."

of the covenant spoke to his barren condition, God promises Abram that his seed will be as many as the stars in the sky.[109]

Family structure is also seen in the scriptures (Ephesians 5:21-33; 6:1-4; 1 Pet 3:1-7).[110] Family structure is set against cultural norms that it may be essentially helpful to impact both this post-modern and pluralistic society. The family provides the basic morals, values, socialization, and ethical and spiritual orientation necessary for an individual to survive in the world.

Family orientation is also responsible for the faith development and the educational environment of their children. The sense of belonging, security, identity, and even overall perspectives on life derive from the family environment.[111] Jan and Myron Chartier, in *Nurturing Faith in the Family*, suggest

> There is an intricate relationship between the family and the church. This relationship has been long recognized within the church. The apostle Paul used

"family" as a key metaphor for thinking about the church as community. God our loving parent; Jesus Christ is our elder brother and we are brothers and sisters in Christ. The family is a primary relational unit in God's family, the Church. The family as a micro-community of faith performs many nurturing functions that are needed in the family of God. If the church is to be strong and serve God's purpose in the world, it needs strong families that nurture its members in belonging, being, believing, benefiting, and becoming.[112]

Family and Extended Family

> "...if African American discipleship is to be successful it must be accomplished through positive kinships and familial relationships."

The African American family in the United States has been continually stereotyped by negative images, particularly by those who are often in the position to make policy and programmatic decisions that have a direct impact on the lives of Black families.[113] Yet, despite the negative mythology and conceptions surrounding the African American family, if African American discipleship is to be successful it must be accomplished through positive kinships and familial relationships.

Harriette McAdoo notes that there are at least three conceptualizations about African American families and how they differ from non-African American families.[114] One view argues that African American families have their essential nature because of poverty. These families are primarily shaped by the lack of resources and if one removes the barrier of poverty, then there would be a convergence of values and structure between all families.[115] Another perspective holds that African American families have been shaped and molded not only by poverty, but also the experience of slavery and Reconstruction.[116]

The final conceptualization is that African American families are unique because of the remnants of African culture that have been maintained and have adapted to discrimination.[117] What is important here is that the

African American family is most likely an amalgamation[118] of all of these perspectives and as such has overcome the destructive difficulties which have assaulted and attempted to annihilate any strong kinship among African Americans. Therefore, because of the durability of the African American family and its history of overcoming, nurture and strength, it lends itself as an excellent vehicle and healing environment for those men who are lost and needing to be restored.[119]

In order to achieve the discipleship of African American men, one must recognize the vast resources provided by and within the structure of the African American family. This recognition of the necessity and importance of the African American family is no small feat. Many social scientists such as E. Franklin Frazier,[120] Daniel P. Moynihan,[121] Ezra Parks, V. B. Phillips, and Stanley Elkins have all subscribed to the cultural ethnocentric philosophy of the African American family. This is to say that as "a result of the manner in which the Negro was enslaved, the Negro's African cultural heritage has had practically no effect on the evolution of his family in the

United States."[122]

E. Franklin Frazier held that the African American family structure as it related to African American marriage and family patterns, customs, and structures was the consequence of slavery and American culture, not cultural transfers.[123] Frazier is arguing against Melville Herskovits and W. E. B. Du Bois, who reasoned that much of Black life is a continuation of African cultural forms and cultural transfers.

Using the social class theory of Frazier, Moynihan issued a 78-page document under the title, *The Negro Family: The Case for National Action*. This report was a seminal report which consistently noted Frazier's conclusions in an effort to highlight the perceived pathologies of the African American family. Today it is known as the "Moynihan Report" and has been used by many social scientists to argue for the detriment of the African American family and kinship ties.

Moynihan characterized the African American community as having broken families, illegitimacy, matriarchy, economic dependency, an inability to pass armed forces entrance tests, high delinquency and crime.[124] Moynihan placed the cause of these problems on a supposedly broken and a disabled Black family.[125] Dodson notes that immediately following the Moynihan Report several other individuals conducted studies and came to find also that there were serious difficulties in the Black family,[126] and the structural foundations of Black families.

At this juncture, McAdoo raises cautions because studies which concentrated on dysfunctional and disorganized aspects of Black family life have deduced that the typical Black family is fatherless, on welfare, thriftless and overpopulated with illegitimate children.[127] Thus it would (according to these studies) necessitate the saving of the Black family from its own pathology.

The Moynihan Report notes clearly that there was still much disparity in America as it relates to class, race and opportunity.[128] In 1965, Moynihan noted several issues relating to the breakdown of African American families. First, the racist virus in the American bloodstream still afflicted the nation.[129] Areas of personal prejudice, mistreatment and even collective empowerment where areas which had been blighted by the holocaust suffered by African Americans. Second, Moynihan posits that over three centuries of harsh abuse have shown themselves in the ability of African Americans to compete on equal footing with others.[130] There is a noticeable theme running through Moynihan's thinking which suggests that things in the Black family were getting considerably worse and not better. Unfortunately, the majority culture could not grasp this fact.

The cure for this supposedly broken family structure appears to be in Moynihan's belief that because the major issue here for African Americans was not class, oppression, racism, or the lack of opportunity, but family structure. A national action plan could assist in rebuilding the African American family. This national action plan would confront both the poor family structure of African Americans and other families within the nation.

This report points to the urban ghettos as tangible proof that the African American family was crumbling.[131] Moynihan argues for a national effort which would stop the cycle of poverty and disadvantage, and strengthen the African American family structure. Although I do not concur with the idea that the major problem with the African American community is the structure (or lack of it) in African American families, one sees that Moynihan was correct in realizing that the cycle of ignorance, poverty, non-opportunity, oppression, racism and job skills would eventually become America's liability and create even greater problems for the African American family and community.

  Moynihan notes that almost twenty five percent of inner city marriages are dissolved, twenty five percent African American births were to unwed mothers, and one-fourth of the African American families were headed by females.[132] Because of these issues, the African American family had begun a massive breakdown--the result of this breakdown would be a pointed increase in welfare dependency. One is encouraged to ask what the root of the problem is from Moynihan's perspective.

  Moynihan lists the six areas in which one can locate the problems of the African American family. Five of these areas are important to understand the dynamics within the African American family as it relates to economics. First, Moynihan notes that unlike other forms of slavery which provided for slaves an ontological location as "human," under religious or legal understanding, American slavery did not recognize captive Africans as anything other than chattel property. As chattel property, there was no recognition (religious or legal) of personhood, marriage, children and certainly no protection for a man's wife. A slave's children or spouse could be sold away without the slave having any legal course of action.[133] This denial of personhood and God given freedom to be human still continues to plague African American families in areas such as self-worth, identity issues of trust and psychological inferiority.

The second aspect was the Reconstruction understanding of freed African captives. Moynihan notes that African captives were given their freedom, but not their equality. This goal was a target of the Jim Crow laws in the ninetieth century. African women were not a threat to the slave master, so these segregation laws targeted the captive African men.[134] The idea was to "keep the Negro in his place." Moynihan cites this principle as a major deterrent to the strong father model.[135] The result of this action was to bring about the emergence of the strong or dominant woman.

Urbanization was noted as the third factor influencing the structural failure of African American families. Moynihan suggests that the rationale for the development of urban slums originated in the swift transition of African American persons from a rural culture to an urban culture and away from persons related to them in their rural culture. This transition would give rise to the development of urban slums. Many African Americans came to the North (cities) and failed to receive the promise of the city. In the rural areas, family pathologies such as divorce, separation and desertion, female family head, children in broken homes, and illegitimacy were lower than in the cities, because of the support system derived from the extended family orientation in the South.[136]

The next area discussed is unemployment and poverty. Here Moynihan utilizes Edward W. Bakke's six stages of adjustment. Stage one and two show the exhaustion of credit and the wife having to enter the work force.[137] The third stage brings into the home a social worker, usually a woman to assist the family. The man is reduced to an errand boy while two women now control the provision for the home.[138] The man (male head of the house) suffers an identity crisis relating to his ability to provide for his home and his family. Moynihan asserts that in America there has been an urgent issue with African Americans getting jobs that could help secure and support their families. This is a major concern because as jobs become more and more available, the African American family becomes stronger and more stable. However, the more difficult jobs were to be found, the more difficult stability and strength was to maintain.[139]

      The wage system was the fifth aspect discussed in relationship to the destruction of the African American family. The wage system in America as a whole does not provide a satisfactory income for struggling couples and families.[140] This is particularly true for African Americans because the study reports that family income is lower for families with children and it was reported that African

American families have more children and have them younger.[141] This data would suggest that because African American families have the largest number of children and the lowest incomes, many African American men cannot adequately support their families.[142]

Andrew Billingsley has been a tremendous corrective for Frazier et al. His research has challenged the pathological, dysfunctional and dependent stereotype that has been a common misperception about the African American family's nurture, functional ability and structure. Billingsley has suggested that two-thirds of African American families living in metropolitan areas are headed by husbands with their wives. Half have managed to pull themselves into the middle class and nine-tenths are self-supporting.[143]

The second school of thought, the cultural relativity school, holds that the African American family is a functional entity.[144] This school builds on the works of Melville Herskovits. Persons such as Andrew Billingsley, Virginia Young, Robert Hill and Wade Nobles argue that the culture of African Americans is uniquely different from that of European Americans. A major tenet of this school is that African American cultural orientation encourages family patterns that are instrumental in combating the oppressive racial conditions of American society.[145]

  Herskovits, unlike Moynihan and Frazier, does not link the difficulties in the African American community to the broken and unstable African American family. Herskovits found what he considered to be authentic African cultural patterns reflected in language, music, art, house, structure, dance, traditional religion, and healing practices.[146] Herskovits saw a relationship between the family life in traditional African societies and that of the African American family in the United States. Herskovits gives a more clear and precise conceptualization and characterization of the family life in traditional African societies as one that has unity, stability and security. It is this positive environment of unity, stability and security which can be utilized for the discipleship of men.

  Dodson highlights the common understanding among the cultural relativist that slavery did not completely destroy (although slavery did distort) the traditional base of

African American family functioning. The African American community is oriented primarily toward extended families. Dodson points to the idea that most African American family structures involve a system of kinship ties.[147] This extended families paradigm is linked by strong kinship ties which affirm the position of the cultural relativist that African American family functioning still exists and shapes to a narrowing degree one's culture and social existence.

> "The concept of kinship and extended family is important to intentional discipleship of African American men."

This extended family system is assumed to provide support for family members either in the form of assistance, protection or for mobility.[148] The concept of kinship and extended family is important to intentional discipleship of African American men. The extended family consists of conjugal and blood relatives, but also non-relatives as well.[149] Extended family relationships interact more with their family according to Hayes and Mendel, particularly in a hostile society. This hostility actually helps to strengthen kinship ties.[150]

The extended family can serve not only as a role model, but also as accountability and responsibility network or system to encourage, nurture and support men that may be struggling to maintain their daily faith. A sense of kinship, belonging and community is of vital importance because from these aspects two benefits emerge. The first benefit is a sense of spiritual and psychological community is provided. The communal aspect is an important piece to assist men in spiritual development and for church belonging, as the church attempts to gain access to pre-Christians and do theology in a "communal" perspective.[151]

The African American extended family paradigm as a resource of liberation, hope, help and healing is essential because the family is a micro model of the church.[152] Also, the extended family is important because it nurtures the necessary relationship of trust which will be mandatory in winning respect in order to gain a hearing from unsaved persons.

The second benefit of "family" modeled discipleship is that within the structure of the extended family there is already present unity, stability, and security. In *Reclaiming The Village: African American Christian Man*, Eddie B. Lane notes that because of the brutal victimization of African American men by a legacy of oppression, cultural brain washing, loss of world view (Christian), and lack of stability or control over the affairs of their personal and public life, the present day African American male needs four things.

1. Holistic spiritual renewal.
2. A renewed sense of trust.
3. A sense of unity in the context of a sense of belonging.
4. A new definition of life.[153]

Lane is correct when he states that fragmented boys grow into fragmented men; persons who do not have a nurturing environment and are pushed into adulthood prematurely will most likely be fragmented by the experience.[154] Again one notes the tremendous importance of the nurturing, extended family environment when seeking social emotional, spiritual, psychological and physical development. Lane reminds the reader that

> Reclaiming the village begins with growing boys into unfragmented men. To this end much attention must be given to the critical three-fold developmental process of male children. This three-fold development emphasizes the boy's physical growth, intellectual development, and reproductive drive. Also important are family and community socialization, the economic context into which the boy is born and grows up and the number of years parents spend growing the boy into a man.[155]

Through discipling men within a kinship and

extended family relationship paradigm and with the assistance of a positive home environment of stability, security, spiritual, psychological and physical development men can be guided into a Christian emphasis and lifestyle change. This process would help to lead African American men into the divine purpose for their lives. Lane states that there is a three-fold purpose to which every man is attached from the moment of conception.

> This three-fold purpose has to do with the internal drive and heart motivation that is nurtured in the boy in the home on his way to manhood. This three-fold purpose consists of the divinely ordained will of men to explore and conquer, combined with the internal motivation to rule over God's creation and the internal drive to reproduce himself.[156]

When African American men and the church can nurture men in an environment which is positive and loving, they will eradicate the negative stereotypes and attitudes such as victim, endangered species, offenders, deadbeat dads or absentee father. Yet, when one is not discipled in this context, African American men will reproduce themselves as victims, endangered species, offenders, and absentee fathers.

> "Discipleship within the framework of the family paradigm would give African American men appropriate role models."

Discipleship within the framework of the family paradigm would give African American men appropriate role models[157] for spiritual maturation and psychological wellbeing (as evidenced through coping skills). This process would teach men the necessity of discipline in matters relating to physical development and satisfaction. Lane advises that in order to facilitate this process discipleship mentors must be able to do at least seven things to realize the goal of the mission of developing men holistically.

1. The effective mentor teaches men how to develop a vocabulary that says what he wants to say in a positive way. This is important as it pertains to the anger felt by black men in helping them express their anger and emotions in a constructive manner. The mentor provides an opportunity for venting in a constructive manner within a constructive environment.
2. The second thing the mentor of black men must do is alter the church program as deemed necessary in order to facilitate the strategy. This alteration might include the order of services,

dress in services, preaching style, small group meetings and transparent modeling of the ministry and the message.
3. The effective mentor of men must be prepared and willing to focus on the protégé's personal life in terms of his character and general attitude. The character of the man has to do with how sound he is in the area of his integrity.
4. The effective mentor must make every effort to discern the attitude of the protégé so that he can determine for himself that what he sees is what others will live with.
5. The mentor must inquire into the professional life of the protégé.
6. The mentor must be personable yet demanding. The mentor should be willing to give the protégé unconditional access and establish a strong tie of accountability.
7. The mentor must be free to challenge the protégé in the areas of morality, marriage, money and ministry.[158]

Robert Joseph Taylor and Waldo E. Johnson, Jr. provide four areas that would be helpful to assist men as it relates to discipleship. The provider role is the first area.[159] One of the areas of difficulty among African American men is the struggle to keep a sense of self-dignity, self-worth, and respect in trying to provide for their family with meager resources and facing great opposition when attempting to attain employment and wages which will be satisfactory to feed their family.

Second, the spousal role is an area where tangible role modeling and accountability is needed. African American men and women tend to marry later than whites. This phenomenon is attributed to the fact that the male partner experiences difficulties in providing for the future of the family. Higher rates of unemployment and under employment and low levels of income among African American men constitute impediments to marriage.[160] Among the most important decisions which influence a couple's decision to marry is the husband's ability to find a job and generate a viable income for the family.[161]

> "Discipleship training must destroy the myth that African American men cannot or are not good fathers."

The instability of African American men has been caused by an inability to provide for their families. Therefore, when an African American man is offered a job which precludes him from worship and Bible study, he is clearly going to accept the job even at the detriment of his spiritual development, soul and family because of his strong determination to be a good spouse and provider.

Still another role is the parental role.[162] Although research in this area has tended to focus on adolescent fathers, out-of-wedlock paternity, or socially vulnerable families, middle class African American fathers are actively involved in the socialization of their children. It has been shown that African American fathers do not appear to be different in their child rearing attitudes from other middle class ethnic groups.[163] Discipleship training must destroy the myth that African American men cannot or are not good fathers. One of the drawbacks of this enterprise is that because of legal separations, divorce or mother-only families, African American men are less likely to live with their biological children.[164] Therefore, it is important to encourage African American men in discipleship training to evidence their commitment to Christ by "being there" and "for" their children.

The last area examined by Taylor and Johnson is the area of family life satisfaction.[165] The authors note that life satisfaction, happiness and morale have grown over the past years.[166] Social and family involvement attributed to this increase in life satisfaction. Family involvement was also linked to satisfactory well-being.[167] This seems to be tangible proof that if African American men are taught and trained within "family" structure, it will not only influence their behavior, well-being and mentality, but also those in their immediate family and their family satisfaction.

> "If discipleship is to lead to Christian maturity it must be done within the confines of a spiritual fellowship..."

Faith: Our Journey In The Church

Careful examination has shown that the African American family, kinship, and extended family paradigm proves to be a sufficient womb for the discipleship of African American men.

However, this discipleship mandate cannot be executed in isolated family or kinship groups. If discipleship is to lead to Christian maturity it must be done within the confines of a spiritual fellowship that is warm, alive and vibrant. It is at this point that the body of Christ, the ecclesia becomes a vital necessity.

Unfortunately, many men have sought to be discipled without the blessed benefit of a warm fellowship to challenge them, hold them accountable and to encourage them in their Christian journey. This may be part of the urgency behind Hebrews 10:23-25.

Let us hold fast the confession of our hope without wavering, for He who promised is faithful; and let us consider how to stimulate one another to love and good deeds, not forsaking our own assembly together as in the habit of some, but encouraging one another, and all the more as you see the day drawing near.

Faith development which leads to Christian maturity must be supported by spiritual communion and commitment with other believers. This seems to be the pattern of the early church as recorded in the ministry of Jesus and book of Acts.[168]

On several occasions the gospels describe how Jesus called the disciples unto himself. Some of these instances were for rest, others for reaching, but all consisted of Jesus' desire for community and fellowship among the disciples (Luke 9:10; Matt 6:30-31; Mark 6:31).

John Scott raises an interesting question, "How would the world Christian situation right now be summed up?" I would describe it as strange, tragic, and possessing a disturbing paradox. In some places it is growing stronger. In others it is characterized by superficiality--the problem is one of growth without depth. In short, the church lacks proper discipleship.[169]

In order to begin the journey toward Christian maturity and faith, one must take serious the discipleship mandate by challenging persons within the faith community to press toward the under emphasized discipline of faith and spiritual development. This sentiment is echoed in Hebrews 5:11-6:2.

> Of whom we have many things to say, and hard to be uttered, seeing ye are dull of hearing. For when for the time ye ought to be teachers, ye have need that one teach you again which be the first principles of the oracles of God; and are become such as have need of milk, and not of strong meat. For every one that useth milk is unskillful in the word of righteousness: for he is a babe. But strong meat belongeth to them that are of full age, even those who by reason of use have their senses exercised to discern both good and evil. Therefore leaving the principles of the doctrine of Christ, let us go on unto perfection; not laying again the foundation of repentance from dead works, and of faith toward God, Of the doctrine of baptisms, and of laying on of hands, and of resurrection of the dead, and of eternal judgment.[170]

If the discipleship mandate is lifted to pragmatic action, it may be necessary for some congregations to shift from program oriented ministries to a Family Ministry approach.[171] This approach is well established in the "helping tradition of the Black Church" and would seek specifically the discipleship and spiritual development of African American men. It would not be exclusive in this goal, but would seek to branch out to all aspects of family life.

Manuel Scott, Sr., Dean of the National Baptist Convention, USA, Christian Education Department and

Pastor Emeritus of the St. John Baptist Church, Dallas, Texas, raises an important question as it relates to Christian discipleship and faith development. If the church and home are to work together in producing mature disciples with a vibrant and developing faith, and if the church is the center of faith training, then when is the church really the church? When is the existential ontology of the church most pure? Using a Pauline theological hermeneutic, Scott argues that the church, if she is to be the faith training center and developer of strong disciples, must first present herself as the "building" of God.[172] First Corinthians 3:9 reads, "For we are labourers together with God: ye are God's husbandry, ye are God's building."

Scott suggests that the church is the property of God and not a human possession. As such she is subject to the authority and commandments of God. This point stands in strength for the discipleship enterprise, in that Paul also argues in Galatians 2:20 and 2 Corinthians 5:15 that believers do not belong to themselves, they have been bought with a price (Rom 6:6; 1 Corinthians 6:19-20). Paul identifies himself as a (*doulos*) servant, slave of God

(Romans 1:1; Phil 1:1, Titus 1:1, Philemon 1:1). He suggests that he is under the authority and command of another Master and that not of himself. Scott develops this idea by quoting Carl Henry. Henry posits that it is Christ who calls the church, Christ who commissions the church and Christ who confirms the church.[173] This is also revealed in Holy Scripture. There is now no condemnation to those who are in Christ Jesus.[174] For those who he foreknew he also predestined to be conformed to the image of his Son, in order that he might be the first born among many brothers. And those whom he predestined he also called; and those whom he called; he also justified; and those who he justified he also glorified.[175]

The second metaphor utilized by Scott is Paul's analogy of the church as Christ's "body"--"Now ye are the body of Christ."[176] Scott notes that if the church presents herself as the "body" of Christ, she will present herself in two aspects: cohesiveness and community. John 17:21 records Jesus' prayer that the disciples (present and future) would be one as Jesus and the Father are one.[177] The attitude of cohesiveness and community are reflected in the actions of service and sacrifice.[178] Because the church exemplifies unity, she can focus on being what she has been called to be. Again, Scott reminds the listener that the public ministry of Jesus was given to the service of humanity. Jesus served with his body in opening blinded eyes, healing the sick, raising the dead, feeding the hungry and opening deaf ears.

> "A theology of discipleship would require one to live in a community of faith and guard the unity of the fellowship."

The second facet mentioned was sacrifice.[179] Scott suggests that the Old Testament and New Testament rest on the shoulders of those who sacrificed themselves for the kingdom.[180] Jesus was the Old Testament "suffering servant" in Isaiah (especially 52:13-53:12) and the sacrificial lamb of the New Testament (John 1:29). He pressed his body into service and sacrifice.[181]

As the church presents this theology of Jesus, believers can access and acquaint themselves with the pragmatic principles of the gospel. One can see that to be a disciple is to work toward making the John 17:21 prayer of Jesus a reality. A theology of discipleship would require one to live in a community of faith and guard the unity of the fellowship. With the blessing of unity comes the burden of service and sacrificial suffering undergirded by absolute surrender (Ephesians 5:1, 2; Phil 2:1-5).

The final aspect lifted by Scott is that the church is the "bride" of Christ. Husbands love your wives as Christ loved the church and gave himself for her.[182] Scott notes here that Romans 7 picks up on this theological pattern by suggesting that Jesus is married to the church and out of this relationship fruit should be produced. Revelation 22:17 is used to further underscore the importance of the church's relationship to Jesus.[183] The theology of this perspective seems to lend itself to the clear understanding that the Christian disciple's life and destiny are interconnected and intertwined with the providence and provision of Jesus. John 15:1-17 is helpful at this point to underscore the relationship of the Master to his disciples. The disciples' productivity, joy, cleansing, friendship, and fruit are dependent on the vine.

Scott correctly asserts that when the church is the church, she presents herself as the 'building", "body" and "bride" of Christ. Thus, the disciple is able to receive and share what Scott calls an evangelical faith.[184]

Challenges

As the African American church moves into the twenty-first century, she must through prayer and the guidance of the Holy Spirit formulate an agenda which takes into major consideration the necessary reform, retooling and broad redirection of the church's focus and energy. The emphasis must be shifted from growth in terms of numbers (membership) to growth in terms of spiritual depth (discipleship). Andrew Billingsley, in *Mighty Like A River: The Black Church and Social Reform*, raises an important question for the African American church to consider.

> The question for the future is this: Can the black church garner enough strength from its rich, fruitful past and its struggles in the present against widespread social turmoil to lead the African American community into a viable future? As the year 2000 approaches, there are strong indications all over the nation that black people will face major challenges.[185]

Billingsley has provided an important point of reference for the agenda of the African American church.

Billingsley points to the dilemma of what the African American church will do with "the urgency of now".[186] In order for the African American church to make the most of "the urgency of now," she must aggressively address the challenges of both today and tomorrow. This action is required because ever evolving are the challenges of being a Christian fellowship that meets the needs of members and society. Ever necessary is reflection upon the church's ability to keep pace with the challenges.[187] If the church is to respond in a manner which glorifies God, she must give strong reflection to the issue of compromise which centers in humanity's sinful and fragmented living.

Billingsley also questions the progressive movement of the African American church in four areas. Each of these areas raise significant concerns for the discipleship of African American men. Some may even be a hindrance rather than a help.

> 1.The challenge is how to move resolutely into recognition, celebration, teaching, and learning of the African American cultural heritage while maintaining and expanding the understanding and practice of the concepts of Christianity that have

83

made the black church the strong institution it is today.

2. A second challenge is how to move the church resolutely into the community, confronting the major social, economic, and political problems, while maintaining and strengthening its primary spiritual mission.

3. The third challenge is to be as contemporary as the morning news, and as ancient as the church itself. How can the black church move resolutely into the acceptance of women as fully equal to men with all the rights and obligations of church stewardship, including the highest offices available?

4. How does the church pursue effectively the first three objectives while maintaining its institutional viability?[188]

Luther Smith asserts that

Their lives are fragmented by the need to serve many different loyalties. Materialism, self-indulgence, cutthroat business practices, and social climbing snare Christians as readily as anyone else in society. Sadly, Christians also often carry these values with them as they conduct the business of the church. The challenge before the church is to shape an identity of discipleship which resists succumbing to values contrary to the Christian faith.[189]

According to Smith, if the church is to be truly a covenant community which emphasizes a new identity (for her members) resulting from radical discipleship and is interested in a viable future, the church must receive a call to listen. The renewal of the church is dependent on its ability to listen.[190] The church can no longer afford to offer the answers to questions that no one is asking. Rather, the church can gain a renewed sense of vision, purpose, and identity from ridding its energies of poor hearing.[191] The church is in need of again coming to distinguish the call of God from the call of other gods.[192] Before the church speaks, the church should engage in prayerful listening.[193] This listening is necessary to keep a strong sense of one's renewal, identity, and calling (Ezekiel 3:15) as well as eliminate the ever present threat of compromise. What is needed is a rekindling of the passion for discipleship.

> "The church can no longer afford to offer the answers to questions that no one is asking."

What are the challenges to discipleship in the African American church particularly among African American men? Smith provides three aspects from the understanding of intentional Christian community which serve as a critique of the church's challenge to disciple

African American men. Smith notes in the preface of his discussion that the word "community" is a translation of the Greek word *koinōnia*. Other meanings of *koinōnia* include "sharing," "communion," or "fellowship."[194] The importance of this aspect of discipleship is seen in the book of Acts among the disciples in the early church. Acts 2:42-47 gives a glimpse of what this fellowship resembled.

> And they devoted themselves to the apostles' teaching and fellowship, to the breaking of bread and the prayers. And fear came upon every soul; and many wonders and signs were done through the apostles. And all who believed were together and had all things in common; and they sold their possessions and goods and distributed them to all, as any had need. And day by day, attending the temple together and breaking bread in their homes, they partook of food with glad and generous hearts, praising God and having favor with all the people. And the Lord added to their number day by day those who were being saved.

Smith is correct in his argument that the communal life is the proper response to being new persons in the name of Jesus.[195] This fellowship which included sharing was the clear pattern for Christian discipleship.[196]

The call to community contains three aspects according to Smith. First, Christians are called to be a peculiar people. This concept is rooted in a religious vision that is formed in the biblical revelation of Jesus' life and ministry.[197] A fellowship which expresses this vision must be formed because Christian faith is best nurtured and made manifest in the context of an intimate fellowship.[198] It is within the nurture of this fellowship that the vision is given a tangible demonstration of the meaning, purpose, and power of faith.[199] Lastly, the Christian fellowship should encourage members to care for one another and for those who are outside the community.[200] This is to suggest that as Christians, disciples are to replicate the ministry of Jesus. Jesus spent his life and his work comforting, reconciling, and liberating sinners, the poor and oppressed.[201]

The call to community contains a second aspect which is finding a particular place.[202] The disciples and their mission are tied to a particular place. It is from this point of reference that the disciples receive their identity.

"disciples are to replicate the ministry of Jesus."

Location is not incidental; rather it is a crucial factor in the community's reason for being.[203] The ministry of disciples and disciple makers must be located in a geographical place in order to build relationships and transform their surroundings (Matt 5:13-16; Rom 12:1,2).

The final aspect of the call to community is that a disciple is one who is called to serve God through intimate fellowship and mission. Such an invitation, however, is not a blueprint which outlines the specifics of a community's work, nor is there the assurance of success.[204] Yet, because discipleship of African American men must be accomplished in a one on one relationship of intimacy, it is necessary for African American men to grasp the biblical importance of covenant and intimacy within the discipleship construct. This means that men come to understand and seek the proper methods for fulfilling the desire to be known and loved. Smith asserts that intimacy in a congregation does not mean that each individual is intimate with every member, but that each individual has a caring involvement with someone or a group of members.[205] Men must covenant with each other to be "present" in the lives of other men for better or worse.

> The church . . . is called to be a fellowship totally committed to increasing understanding and deepening relationships that empower Christian discipleship. The absence of intimacy within a congregation may impair its ability to nurture members in understanding the meaning of covenant in a Christian fellowship and in the Christian faith.[206]

The imperative in Matthew 5:13-16 is unquestionably an imperative which points the believer to a cruciform existence that is contrary to the culture and condition of sinful humanity. However, there remain many challenges which have tended to impede the development, growth and spiritual maturity of the saints. Smith argues that the challenge before the church is to shape an identity of discipleship which resists succumbing to values contrary to the Christian faith. In doing this, the church need not attempt to isolate its members from modernity and society, but it should help them to be a prophetic witness to culture. Christian disciples are a peculiar people. They celebrate being in this world, yet they are a peculiar people who are not of it.[207]

T. Vaughn Walker, in Black Church Strategies for the Twenty-First Century, notes that Sid Smith is correct in realizing that unless the African American churches' agenda has family ministry as a major emphasis-- the ministry of the church will be irrelevant and ineffective.[208] This idea is a helpful critique in that it underscores the importance of the discipleship enterprise being located in the home. This challenge to discover, define and duplicate Christian disciples is not only a congregational priority, but a priority of primary importance for the home. Again, it is necessary for the African American church to grasp this construct and understand both historically and today its role as one which addresses all aspects of human existence.[209]

> "...before the church is to shape an identity of discipleship which resists succumbing to values contrary to the Christian faith."

Walker articulates the importance and continued emphasis on the African American church as the pacesetter and model for freedom and community. It has been the only institution in the African American community that has said, at least in theory, "whosoever will, let them come."[210] In this area of theology, Walker points to James Cone's four concerns or themes that the African American church must be mindful of: "sexism, the exploitation of the Third World, classism, and an inordinate methodological dependence upon the neo-orthodox theology of Karl Barth and other European theologians."[211] The African American churches' mandate is to address each of these areas from the standpoint of a cruciform discipleship. Only the church has the power to bring forth the godliness that must accompany freedom and liberation. The African American community will never realize ultimate freedom and liberation if it does not stay committed to Jesus Christ and His church.[212]

With the many paradigm shifts that are presently occurring within American society and culture, the African American church is challenged to become more creative and innovative in areas such as holistic involvement in family life and development, teenage pregnancy, basic morality, economic empowerment, community networking, Christian education, adoptive homes for children, curriculum, rites of passage, singles ministry, marriage ministry, equipping, alcoholics anonymous-narcotics anonymous, politics, mentoring, sexuality and staffing.[213]

> "..some ministries are attempting to disciple persons using "Model-T" resources in an e-mail/internet era."

There are many multifaceted challenges facing any congregation that seeks to shift from a mere membership driven congregation to a discipleship driven congregation. The challenges to be discussed are not intended to be the exhaustive or by any means the "final" word, however, they are areas that have surfaced in discussion groups, research, or in the preaching – teaching ministry of senior ministers.

One of the most important challenges facing urban ministries and congregations is the lack of proper facilities and urban demise. Discipleship focuses the believer on relationships which are structured around Jesus the Christ in prayer, worship, ministry, maturity and fellowship, but for these areas to become fruitful – the church must have a facility that lends itself to proper environment and equipment. Unlike suburban or mid-city churches, urban churches were built between the late 1800's and early twentieth century. This means that some ministries are attempting to disciple persons using "Model-T" resources in an e-mail/internet era. Proper facilities are important when one considers that churches built in the late 1800's were not equipped with even the proper electrical circuitry to run copy machines, soda machines, or overhead projectors without blowing fuses. These older facilities often cannot accommodate congregations who have grown in numbers, and now seek to disciple the new converts. Many urban congregations cannot afford to build, therefore, they are forced to focus on extra giving opportunities not for the purpose of discipleship materials for ministry, but to maintain or repair aging buildings.

Another area of difficulty is caused when the African American church changes their discipleship paradigm from a preaching exclusive paradigm to a staff or ministry discipleship paradigm.[214] Because of the lack of financial resources and the geographical and socio-economic landscape of urban ministry, urban churches have great difficulty adding full or part-time staff. Volunteers are utilized and for a time this is sufficient. However, volunteers are just that, volunteers. Although they are assisting, they cannot really be held to the same expectations and standards as persons who are on staff. This presents a grave dilemma for the church. Either the pastor is asked (or knows) to meet the unfulfilled needs or they go unmet. To those urban pastors who are bi-vocational or in some instances tri-vocational this means important ministry needs are left lacking.

Stewardship and stewardship education have not been emphasized by and large in the African American church. As a result of the lack of teaching many churches have resorted to the selling of dinners, fish fry's, and various contests in order to support the work of the church. Socio-economic conditions and contextual injustices have also contributed to the phenomena. Although the desire and motive of these fund raising ideas are admirable, the scriptures teach the holistic practice of stewardship.[215] The discipleship of men must include the exegesis and explanation of what it means to be responsible, accountable, and a good manager of all of God's blessings. This teaching must not be focused extensively on just one area, rather it must be holistic, that is to suggest it should extend to all parts of one's Christian living. Each disciple must prove faithful in their biblical understanding and application of stewardship principles so that church resources do not go to a few staff or clergy.[216]

Walker provides five serious challenges for the African American church in the next century and these challenges directly affect the discipleship enterprise. First, Walker examines the issue of diversity within area churches and denominations.[217] Loyalty as it relates to churches and denominations is not as strong a concern as it once was in previous generations. The power of individual choice is much greater and cultural sensitivity is seen as an important aspect in minority communities. When one considers the research which notes the spiritual hunger in America, it is important to note that churches must provide a product which entices humanity to "come and see."

The second challenge rests in the ethical dimension of faith.[218] Walker provides several questions which speak to this challenge. What to think about birth control, what view of abortion to hold, how Christians should comport themselves in the workplace, what the best curriculum would be for instructing young people how to think ethically, and so on are major ethical issues that need to be addressed by African American churches.[219] Walker is correct in pointing to the fact that the African American church has long been an ethnically conservative organism, while seeking to be socially relevant and progressive in ministry.[220] It especially is important to help men understand and apply the ethical mandates of scripture and to be able to live what they hold as important lifestyle convictions (1 Tim 6:14, 4:12, 4:15-16; 2 Tim 1:12-14) if they are to be mature disciples of Jesus the Christ.

The third area mentioned is the problem of belief.[221] What is the appropriate relationship between African American Christians and the Nation of Islam?[222] One of the difficulties represented here is

> "...the job of African American disciple making churches is to bring a Christ distinctive to the daily living of these men."

that many African American men want a syncretistic religion. They desire a buffet of all that several religions have to offer. African American men are attracted to the suits and ties of the Nation of Islam brothers, as well as their discipline and numbers, but they still desire to experiment with Buddhism, philosophy and "momma's church." Therefore, the job of African American disciple making churches is to bring a Christ distinctive to the daily living of these men. Holy Scripture is clear on this doctrinal point that Jesus, God's only begotten Son is the only way to the Father and salvation (John 14:6; 15:1-8; Acts 4:12, Rom 10:9,10).

Another aspect of this doctrinal concern is the relationship of the African American church and the largely white conservative religious right. The issue of difficulty for Walker is how far apart these two groups remain and the fact that they continue to grow in distance from each other.[223] If a component of discipleship is to seek reconciliation (2 Corinthians 5:18-19), then this is a very problematic issue for the church at large. Walker is correct in his assessment of the word "conservative" as utilized by

African Americans and white Christians. Yet, each group has much in common with the other and this common agreement should assist in bringing about the necessary healing and helping that is required by both.

The next challenge is the public role of Christianity.[224] These public role issues or political concerns arise as people of faith seek to display or practice their faith on behalf of the marginalized, dispossessed, disenfranchised, least, lost and left out. The African American church was at the forefront in the Civil Rights struggle, and African American clergy persons were leading the charge. Is this still necessary and if so how does being a Christian disciple mandate our activism on behalf of the kingdom of God? A helpful response to this question must be founded upon how the Old Testament prophets warned God's people about injustices and also the manner in which Jesus revealed God's love and grace for those who were victims of oppression (Micah 6:8; Amos 5:24; Matt5; Jas 1:27). Disciples are called to be obedient fruit producers and this calling is most apt when a disciple is working in the midst of wrong to make it right or working in the midst of darkness to bring light.

Incarnational discipleship seeks to bring the presence of God upon the negative circumstance in order that transformation may occur. Glenn Stassen, in his article Incarnating Ethics, notes the importance of incarnational ministry in the number of times Jesus confronted persons in the gospel of Luke.

> "Incarnational discipleship seeks to bring the presence of God upon the negative circumstance in order that transformation may occur."

Nine times Jesus confronted people for not showing love in their actions. Nine times he confronted folks for their greed and hoarding, which get in the way of single-minded service toward God and loving action toward the needy. Nine times Jesus confronts people for having divided loyalties, rather than serving God alone. Eight times he confronted people for showing by their actions that they did not recognize his authority. Eight times he confronted people who were seeking places of honor and reputation, and urged instead the way of servant-like humility. Seven times he emphasized that the crucial question is whether we actually do what he teaches, versus the hypocrisy of claiming to be on the side of righteousness while not doing God's will. Seven times he called people explicitly to repent, to take the log out of our own eye, to stop being self-righteously critical of others and insisting on our own way, and instead to be more humble and loving toward him and toward others.[225]

The final challenge given by Walker addressed the personal lives of the believers themselves.[226] He notes that despite frequent accusations that Americans are greedy, shallow and self-centered, much evidence exists that for the most part people want to be good.[227] Walker sees a relationship at this point between the black extended family and the black church. It is a correct assertion that in some sense, the African American church is the best model and paradigm of extended family and support in the Christian faith. At this point, Walker points to the fact that the black church was the first black school, the primary carrier of black folk culture, the pacesetter for values which are positive and affirming, the vehicle for complete and holistic liberation (freedom and confederation)[228] and also a communal place of healing. These important and vital results were directly tied to the fact that the persons in the African American church believe that if one truly "had church" it should not only impact their lives, but the lives of others also.

In *A Quest For Freedom: An African American*

Odyssey, Mack King Carter also notes several challenges to the African American church which will impair the discipleship of African American men. Carter advises first that the African American church must redefine its enslavement to the American Way of Life and seek to develop its own people and churches.[229] This is not to suggest any type of volunteer segregation or nationalism, rather there is the need to reformulate the methods and mentality the African American church is using to bring about freedom to her people and community. Carter notes that the church should be focusing on "alternative consciousness."[230] He is arguing for the developing of a lifestyle, and thinking (perception) which runs counter cultural and is grounded in the biblical character of the Christ.[231] This counter cultural lifestyle and thinking is developed by the proclamation of a gospel that is also counter cultural.[232] The end goal of this process or transformation is freedom which as he suggests is both

> "Churches must encourage and empower their members to produce rather than just consume."

imminent and eternal.

Carter calls next for the African American church to overcome her preoccupation with the "sadistic insanity" of biblical and education illiteracy. Carter divides this challenge into four areas: public and private education, college and universities, theological education and laity empowerment education.[233] Carter argues that while each of these areas is helpful, as far as African American's are concerned there are still great gaps which must be filled by the church. One tends to concur with Carter at this point because it has been proven that the higher one's educational level is the more likely one is to be involved in church activities.

A third area of challenge and concern is the need for both "protest and produce" within the African American community and church.[234] Carter asserts that the role of the African American church in the twenty-first century will be to continue to sound the trumpet against the establishment that oppresses the community.[235] This protest involves "sounding the alarm" not only as it relates to evil in one's community, but wherever there is oppression and evil in the world. Protest is not considered an end in itself. Churches must encourage and empower their members to produce rather than just consume. The scriptures speak clearly to this issue of Christian production. Jesus says in Matthew 5:16, "Let your light so shine, that they may see your good works and glorify your Father which is in heaven."[236] John 15:8 records Jesus saying, ""My Father is glorified by this, that you bear much fruit and become my disciples."[237] The African American church should instruct men to protest injustice everywhere, yet one lives to bring forth fruit (Gal 5:22) that is befitting a mature Christian disciple.

The final concern lifted by Carter is the tension between the priestly and prophetic roles in the African American church being priestly and prophetic. In some sense disciples are called to be both an Amaziah (Amos 7:10-13) and an Amos (Amos 7:14-17). Carter notes that the church does not choose one above another, or one to the exclusion of the other. Both are indispensable in the authentic church.[238] As priests, the African American Christian disciple is the voice of those who have been marginalized. We are to show compassion--genuine concern and helpfulness to the best of their abilities.[239] As prophet, the believer must cry like the gospel globetrotter, the apostle Paul--"the wages of sin is death, but the gift of God is eternal life" (Romans 6:23).

Andrew Billingsley, in *Mighty Like a River: The Black Church Social Reform Black Church and Social Reform,* notes that if the African American church is to be successful in the coming days, the African American church must re-tool for a new generation.[240] The African American church should assist in providing more than just salvation for the soul, she must strengthen both the head and the mind. Billingsley notes five areas to work toward.

1. Provide a more equitable place for women in all levels of leadership of the churches;
2. Provide strong incentives for men to participate in organized church sponsored programs;
3. Use their enormous financial and economic power in the interest of (holistic) social reform;
4. Honor, learn, and teach African American heritage as a major component of their mission; and
5. Have and harness their recognized political power to deliver sounder public policies and private programs to their communities – before, during, and after elections, and in non-electoral politics as

well.[241]

Some pragmatic challenges to African American men being discipled also were given to me by the Men's Ministry of Galilee Baptist Church.

1. No role models (overall).

2. No role models which translated mature Christian discipleship into daily living.

3. Lack of older, established African American men to assist younger men in the dealing with daily struggles of being "transformed."

4. Raised in the tradition of just going to worship and not having or expecting to receive something from worship.

5. Crisis driven relationship with God.

6. Teachings did not emphasize a change in character.

7. Saw a Christian not behaving as a Christian either in the church or on the streets.

8. Fear of the cost of being a disciple.

9. Not ready to give up everything.

10. Did not want to follow a soft, white suburban Jesus.

11. Too busy with my own life.

12. No emphasis in teaching on intentional prayer, life change, expectations, Bible study, holiness and repentance.

13. Failure as an identity.

14. Failure translating into self-hatred.

15. Shame of ones' self because they did not have it altogether.

16. Lack of a "close" relationship or father figure.

17. Christianity presented as too feminized.

18. Peer pressure <u>not</u> to change or be involved in church.

19. Feelings of disconnectedness from "the experience" in church (crying, shouting and praising)

20. Unable to grasp "Jesus" because of cultural identification – Jesus does not identify with who, what, and where I am in the daily struggle of urban life. Jesus does not "look" like me. [242]

As difficult as the challenges are the future of the black church depends heavily on their constructive resolutions. To this we will turn in chapter 3.

CHAPTER 3

MODELS OF MINISTRY

Discipleship is not a one size fits all enterprise within the body of Christ. There should flexibility and fluidness in how one disciple's a person within a particular context or a particular congregation of people. This seems to be one of the mistakes made in discipleship in the contemporary church. Either there is no ministry of discipleship or persons are being force fed the same methods of discipleship. James Houston, a leading evangelical senior theologian of spiritual life, provides significant insights into the church's inability to make disciples. Houston notes first that disciple making is not just about replicable, transferable methods, but about the mystery of two walking together.[243] He further states that methods treat discipleship as a problem to be solved, but mentoring treats discipleship as a relationship to be lived.[244] Houston posits

> "Discipleship is not a one size fits all enterprise within the body of Christ."

that one is incorrect to consider Christian maturity as anything other than shared social reality. "Christian maturity is always a social, and never an individual reality. There is no such thing as my maturity. There is only our maturity."[245] While one agrees that Christian maturity occurs in the womb of Christian fellowship and community, one would also be so quick to argue that this Christian maturity is at some point an individual pursuit in the midst of a Christian community with the same goal or prize.

Another important insight given by Houston is that the primary pressure militating against effective disciple-making (in the context of accountable relationship) is the contemporary tendency toward reductionism, which places a premium on thought, emphasizes the rational over the mysterious, and operates in an utilitarian mode. Thus, we manipulate reality so we can live by methodology.[246] This is a vital statement because it sheds light upon the need for a balanced approach to discipleship. One should know with their head and know (*yada*) with their hearts as well. Reductionism which emphasizes prayer and Bible study, but gives little consideration to other areas of spiritual discipline such as meditation, examination of conscience, intercession, solitude, works of kindness (mercy), preaching, baptism, the Lord's Supper, the kingdom of God, the role of the Spirit and the assurance of the believer's remaining in Christ must be avoided.[247]

> "...discipleship is a process that takes place within accountable relationship over a period of time.."

Within this framework, the consultation's official statement defining discipleship is helpful--discipleship is a process that takes place within accountable relationship over a period of time for the purpose of bringing believers to spiritual maturity in Christ.[248] One can see that discipling involves at least three components: it must be done in relationship, it happens over a period of time, and it has as its goal the spiritual maturity and equipping of the saints (Ephesians 4:13-16). A fourth component would be the conviction of obedience in the believer's daily life.

John Stott and Tokunboh Adeyemo call attention to at least two other methodological concerns relating to the insufficient effort on the part of churches to disciple their converts. First, Stott notes that evangelical Christians commit the moral equivalent of child abuse when they pour all their energies into evangelistic programs and fail to make sure that spiritual newborns are given the nurture they need to grow into healthy, mature followers of Jesus.[249] The church would do well to assign each new believer a mature disciple who could assist in helping the new convert through an open relationship to become rooted and grounded in their new lifestyle. Stott advises that this type of mentor model is always efficient, but is essential to our growing in grace.[250] This is one of the critical areas that must be addressed in the discipling of African American men. We have noted in the previous chapter the very necessity and urgency of having an incarnational, tangible presence in the form of an older, mature brother to help men realize the presence of the Holy in their lives. It appears that Stott has pointed the church to one of the reasons our churches have become so

> "The church would do well to assign each new believer a mature disciple who could assist in helping the new convert..."

superficial and Stott calls over this a "strange and disturbing paradox". The church has experienced enormous statistical growth without corresponding growth in discipleship.[251]

African theologian Tokumboh Adeyemo grieves this same "strange and disturbing paradox" concerning Africa as well, when he states that the church in Africa is one mile long, but one inch deep. What is needed are visions and models of discipling which embrace the idea of accountable relationship within the womb of church or Christian fellowship and which will invest time to bring believers into a spiritual maturity exemplified through obedience. Adeyemo is correct in his assertion that discipleship "is not information, but character formation."[252] Without an appropriate vision or model of discipling those who come to Christ, the church misses the goal of Jesus to make "disciples" (Matt 28:18-20). Stott argues that if the church offers evangelism without

> "..if the church offers evangelism without discipleship or disciple-making, she is guilty of offering cheap grace, not God's grace."

discipleship or disciple-making, she is guilty of offering cheap grace, not God's grace. It would be like a wedding without a marriage, a celebration without substance.[253] Although the key issues for discipleship may be different depending on the context of a particular people, the core need remains the same. Urban churches of America may need to focus on such issues as appropriate facilities, funding, violence, educational programs, economic empowerment, materialism, self-hatred, teenage pregnancy or hedonism; while suburban churches in America may need to examine issues of greed, pride, arrogance, envy, materialism, prejudice and corruption. Context determines the particulars in the issues to be addressed. Appianda Arthur gives an important consideration when he notes, "in each culture, discipleship must wear its own face."[254]

As the African American Church begins to explore various models and ministries of discipleship, she must first define the goal of Christian maturity and discipleship as it relates to African American men. Fred Luter, pastor of Franklin Avenue Baptist Church in New Orleans, Louisiana has ten goals for an effective men's ministry that will reach and minister to African American men. These goals are:

1. To help men grow spiritually.
2. To prepare men to become the priest of their homes.
3. To show men how to love their wives as Christ loved the church.
4. To show fathers how to produce godly children.
5. To help equip other men in the church.
6. To help win other men to the Lord.
7. To lighten the counseling load of the pastor.
8. To develop accountability among other men.
9. To develop future church leaders.
10. To develop role models and mentors for our teens and children.[255]

These goals can be broken down into five categories: (1) spiritual nurture, (2) development, (3) relational development, (4) counseling, and (5) accountability. Disciple models that incorporate these aspects will attract men who seek to encounter authentically the Christ and allow him to eradicate all things and make all old things new (2 Corinthians 5:17).

Another implicit goal of reaching African American men through the African American church is to help those in the congregation understand and take ownership of the heritage of the African American church as the historical and existential source of both spiritual and physical liberation. Many African American men do not know the historical importance, relevance, and heritage of the African American church, nor do they understand what the church is doing presently to liberate her community spiritually and physically.

Eddie B. Lane gives several aspects to assist African American men in understanding the past and present necessity of the African American church. First, Lane points to the important contribution of being a viable carrier of black culture.[256] The African American church is a viable organism for reaching African American men because she has proven herself a faithful steward of African culture and people. Lane notes that the Black church is the mother and sustainer of Black culture.[257]

> "..the Black church is the mother and sustainer of Black culture."

Another important facet of the church's viability to reach African American men is her ability to assist persons in maintaining their psychological liberation through the worst of times, and in maintaining a sense of "community village" and ontological personhood.[258] This sense of community and identity gives rise to stable families, educational opportunities, economic opportunities and networking.

      Lane goes on to argue that once the goal and aim of men's ministry is defined and the church is affirmed as a viable means through which to reach, evangelize and disciple men, the next area of study would be the obstacles to reaching African American men. The first obstacle to examine would be the disdain for the African American preacher by African American men.[259] Some African American men have a passionate hatred for the African American preacher which appears to be a result of the psychological and mental lynching which occurred during slavery. Lane notes that negative attitudes of African American men towards the African American preacher is perhaps more related to the assault of the media, entertainment and the majority race on the integrity of the African American male leadership in general.[260] According to Lane, historically persons in the South attempted to kill or destroy African American preachers in an attempt to control the African American community. When killing African American ministers became ineffective, those in the South with power began to kill the influence of the African American minister/leader with claims of immorality and thievery.[261] An excellent example of this type of mental lynching is cited by Lane when he discusses the moral assault on Martin L. King, Jr. by the Federal Bureau of Investigation.[262] How can African American men be discipled in close relationship to the pastor, if the pastor is perceived as an enemy to their individual and corporate liberation?

The second barrier to reaching African American men effectively is the legacy of Eurocentric theology.[263] Many African American men and scholars have noted the detriment of White theology in the African American community.[264] It has not been the gospel of Jesus Christ that African Americans have had issue with, rather historically it has been the interpretation and application of the gospel that has been problematic. Because of this gap in interpretation and especially application of the gospel,

Lane is correct to assert,

> The effective evangelization of black men requires a message that is relevant to the African American male context and liberating in its focus in terms of Black culture, spirit, and lifestyle. This emphasis on preaching a liberating gospel as opposed to a gospel that is stoic, restrictive or passive in no way suggests that the content of the gospel is to be changed. It is the application of the gospel that must be changed-- adapted to the African American male context.[265]

The third barrier to be taken into consideration is the perception that the gospel is a gospel of passivity.[266] Ministers must stand bold and declare God to be a God of action, even a God of aggressive activity. God must not be allowed to become a God of non-action and God must not be feminized or given attributes that position one's perception of God to be overly weak, timid and limited. God must be a God who gave his only begotten Son Jesus to the world to bring about victory over Satan, sin, and the oppressive and evil world systems. The gospel of Jesus is generally preached to black men in words that cause it to be perceived as a message of restrictions, limitations, barriers, and even oppression.[267] African American ministers and pastors must be bold and preach the gospel message with power, authority and in a passionate manner to reach African American men.

The last barrier noted by Lane is the lack of leadership positions for men in the church.[268] Women appear to be in dominance in most leadership responsibilities in the African American church. No doubt this may have something to do with the fact that because men have not been in church consistently, leadership positions have been given to those who were actually there. Lane provides two solutions to assist with this concern.

> "..an effective discipleship ministry to black men is to develop holistically each man in the group.."

> The effective pastor in the arena of Black male ministry is one who is himself a man among men in his physical fitness, discipline, lifestyle and overall self-management. Second, he is a man who surrounds himself with men who are his equals in every way and even his superior in many ways. The effective pastor is a man with a vision and a burden for real men: yet he does not exclude women from leadership in the ministry.[269]

The church must help to provide the atmosphere

118

in teaching and worship to move in the direction of intentional discipleship of African American men and understand the goal of an effective discipleship ministry to black men is to develop holistically each man in the group to his maximum potential in Jesus Christ. The heart of such a goal is a strategy of evangelism that has at its core evangelism and discipleship.[270] If the church does this, she will bring forth not only mature disciples, but also men who are productive workers.

The Model of Empowerment

Robert Stein, Mildred Hogan Professor of New Testament at the Southern Baptist Theological Seminary in his article, *Baptism and Becoming a Christian in the New Testament*, notes that

> In the New Testament, conversation involves five integrally related components or aspects, all of which took place at the same time, usually on the same day. These five components are repentance, faith, and confession by the individual, regeneration, or the giving of the Holy Spirit by God, and baptism by representatives of the Christian community.[271]

Unfortunately once African American men have

come to Christ and been converted, confessed, repented, been regenerated and baptized, they seem to fall through the cracks or quickly find the back exit sign. There are several possibilities for these phenomena, and the present focus is on locating pragmatically and theologically models that will eliminate this negative trend.

> "..the mature disciple life is lived as holy wherever life is lived."

Upon being converted to Christ, Matthew 28:20 states "and teaching them to obey everything that I have commanded you." The new people of "the way" were to be taught to obey or observe all that Jesus had commanded. One can raise a serious question with respect to whether this is happening within our congregations.

The model of empowerment looks to this teaching component as the central emphasis in developing mature disciples. If these new African American men converts are to live and walk in the power of God, there are several important aspects of the faith they must understand and affirm. From an "African or Black Sacred Cosmos" cosmology the holy cannot be separated or partitioned out of one's daily existence. There is no division between the secular and the sacred. All of life comes from God and therefore all of life is holy. Thus, for the mature disciple life is lived as holy wherever life is lived. Belief and behavior are not and cannot be separated.[272] Robert Coleman notes that

> Coming to Christ in the early church constituted an engagement of one's total personality and lifestyle. Those who believed were persons "obedient to the faith." God gave His spiritual powers "to them that obey him." Clearly faith involved more than an intellectual assent to the historical validity of Christ's work; as Jesus had said, it was a commitment to follow Him--to walk in His steps.[273]

Another important aspect to be affirmed is that one's obedience brings about a reorientation of one's lifestyle. This reorientation is undergirded by one's faithfulness and continued commitment to count the cost. African American men must come to understand that being a witness, lifestyle reorientation and obedience are not possible in one's own strength, will power or even determination. Acts 1:8 and Luke 24:49 both declare that without the empowerment of the Holy Spirit disciples are ill equipped to fulfill the Great Commission. Many African American men leave or get upset with the church because they fail to realize that the walk of faith is a walk empowered by the Holy Spirit and not works of the flesh. Thus to be empowered in witness, work and word, the disciple must be equipped. Ephesians 4:11-16 is crucial at this point.

> And he gave some, apostles; and some, prophets; and some, evangelists; and some, pastors and teachers; For the perfecting of the saints, for the work of the ministry, for the edifying of the body of Christ: Till we all come in the unity of the faith, and of the knowledge of the Son of God, unto a perfect man, unto the measure of the stature of the fullness of Christ. That we henceforth be no more children,

tossed to and fro, and carried about with every wind of doctrine, by the sleight of men, and cunning craftiness, whereby they lie in wait to deceive; But speaking the truth in love, may grow up into him in all things, which is the head, even Christ: From whom the whole body fitly joined together and compacted by that which every joint supplieth, according to the effectual working in the measure of every part, maketh increase of the body unto the edifying of itself in love.

The disciple should be able to explain and "give a defense for the hope that is in them" (1 Pet 3:15). In order to accomplish this task, the disciple must understand the ministry of the Holy Spirit.

Fred Luter, pastor of Franklin Avenue Baptist Church has suggested that, "without power, we will constantly live defeated lives."[274] If African American men are to become empowered disciples in relationship with the Christ, re-socialized and obedient to Christ's commands, they must grasp the necessity and critical importance of the Comforter (John 14-16).

Luter asserts ten aspects of the work of the Holy Spirit in working with men.

1. Convicts men of sin (John 16:7,8)
2. Regenerates the believer (John 3:5; Titus 3:5)
3. Indwells the believer (1 Corinthians 6:19, 20
4. Seals the believer (Ephesians 1:13-14)
5. Fills the believer (Ephesians 5:18)
6. Empowers the believer (Acts 1:8)
7. Produces fruit in the life of the believer (Gal 5:22, 23)
8. Imparts gifts to the believer (1 Corinthians 12:1-11)
9. Leads the believer (Gal 5:16-18)
10. Teaches the believer (John 14:26)

Luter shows here that the Holy Spirit came to do a work in and through every believer.[275]

This next area of concern may be why so few Christians (especially men) are continually filled with the Spirit. Luter sees five major hindrances in this area as it relates to being filled with the Spirit. The first area is found in Hosea 4:6--a lack of knowledge of the word of God. Second, is the attitude of pride. This aspect is based in Isaiah 14:12-14. Third, many Christians have a phobia or fear of what a relationship with Christ would entail or even are ashamed of their salvation--Luke 9:26. Fourth, Luter notes that one's secret sins may keep them from being filled with the Holy Spirit--1 John 1:9. The last area mentioned by Luter is the worldly-mindedness of the believer. This carnality or carnal mindedness is contrary to the will and word of God.[276] First John 2:15-17 states

> "..if the believer desires an empowered and victorious Spirit filled walk, it is necessary for him to be Christ-like or Spirit controlled.."

> Love not the world, neither the things that are in the world. If any man love the world, the love of the Father is not in him. For all that is in the world, the lust of the flesh, and the lust of the eyes, and the pride of life, is not of the Father, but is of the world. And the world passeth away, and the lust thereof: but he that doeth the will of God abideth forever.

Luter is correct to assert that if the believer desires an empowered and victorious Spirit filled walk, it is necessary for him to be Christ-like or Spirit controlled (Ephesians 5:18) and to give Christ total control of their life (Gal 2:20).[277]

What are the pragmatic steps to empowerment of the believer? According to Luter, there are seven steps to an empowered spiritual life.

> Step 1. Acknowledging Our Need
> John 15:5
> Step 2. Affirming God's Power
> Philippians 4:13
> Step 3. Tapping into the Power
> Ephesians 5:18
> Step 4. Maintaining Christ's Lordship
> I Peter 3:15
> Step 5. Experience Spiritual Cleansing
> 1 John 1:9
> Step 6. Growing in Christ
> Step 7. Serving the Kingdom
> Matthew 28:19-20[278]

African American men who understand the work, accessibility, and transforming power of the Holy Spirit will be on a spiritual journey of maturing in Christ.

The Model of Resocialization

Romans 12:1,2 states "I beseech you, brethren by the mercies of God, that you present your bodies a living sacrifice, holy and acceptable to God, which is your reasonable service. Do not be conformed to this world but be ye transformed by the renewing of your minds that you may prove what is the good and acceptable will of God.

First Corinthians 6:20 continues this idea of being different by virtue of works: "For ye were bought with a price; therefore glorify God in your body." Matthew 5:16; 1 Corinthians 10:31; 1 Peter 1:13-16; 1 Peter 2:9,21; and Romans 12:17ff all point to an ontological distinctiveness about the person who has committed themselves to become a disciple of Jesus. Matthew 5 is a tremendous example of an incarnational ethic working itself out through the life of the believer.

What occurs in many African American men is the struggle of "saved, but not yet there." They believe and genuinely desire to serve, but

> "Resocialization is defined as the process of helping new believers see their citizenship.."

because there may not exist an accountability network or a strong mentor relationship with stronger and older brothers--the young brothers will "lapse" into their old, sinful behaviors.

Resocialization is defined as the process of helping new believers see their citizenship is not on the terrestrial, but on the celestial level, thereby helping them to practice a Christian ethic which embraces the distinctive of being a child of God. This process is holistic in its nature encompassing mind, body and soul.

Dr. Lloyd Blue, retired pastor and staff person at the Concord Baptist Church in Dallas, Texas speaks to the importance of resocialization in the discipleship process when he notes that the church must seek to build relationships with men because many African American men suffer from both the "identity crisis" and "second class citizenship syndrome."[279] Salvation and regeneration must transform how an individual man sees himself in light of the Christ-event. This means that a part of the resocialization process must speak to the questions – "who am I in this world"and "where does my spiritual inheritance intersect with my physical living?" Blue notes that men need to be resocialized to see each other through the eyes of Jesus and not culture.[280] This Christian remobilization and identity pervades not only the individual disciple, but also how men relate to their home life, wife, children, church, and community.

Another important area of resocialization is the self-worth of African American men. Blue advises that churches and pastors who hope to disciple African American men must teach them that they have "treasure in earthen vessels" and share with them the importance of their help to carry the load both at church and in their community. Genesis 1:26; 2:7; Psalm 8; 139:14 all convey the worth of man as God's creation. Yet, many men live subpar as disciples because either they do not know this biblical worth or do not choose to live it out due to negative support systems or negative interpretations of who they are as Christian men.[281]

> "..fragmented men are men who do not like themselves as a whole."

Lane states correctly that the church must seek to develop and nurture "unfragmented" men. How does this come to be?

Lane notes that fragmented men are men who do not like themselves as a whole. It is the fragmentation in this area of their self-esteem (worth) that contributes to overall poor performance of black men in their relationships with their wives and children.[282] Therefore, Lane gives two suggestions for the resocialization of African American men and developing unregimented men. First, he advises that according to Genesis 2:18-25, God gives the pattern and design for developing unfragmented men. This pattern notes that God did not design men to be alone. Men cannot exist in a relational vacuum.[283] African American men in western culture are taught the philosophy of rugged individualism and independence. We see this phenomenon reversed in urban African American men who know the code of street life is one of danger and often join gangs for protection and emotional support, yet the gangs stand against all normal mores of conduct. Unlike many men in the church, these gangs point to the importance of relational resocialization.

> "Morality and ethics are keys to determining the strength of one's discipleship and relationship with the Christ."

Lane's second point is that Adam was created to

reflect the image and glory of God. Thus, the man Adam was created with a moral code by which he was to live.[284] Morality and ethics are keys to determining the strength of one's discipleship and relationship with the Christ. This biblical code of morality should be at the heart of all the African American disciple does and should bring much fruit and glory to God (John 15:8, 16). This biblical morality runs counter to culture, but is upheld in scripture and therefore should take on an incarnational form (John 1:14) in the lifestyle of the disciple. Lane utilizes Ephesians 4:23-24, "to be made new in the attitude of your minds; and to put on the new self-created to be like God in true righteousness and holiness" to give these seven benefits of African American men who have put off the old self, put on the new self, and are renewed in the spirit of their minds.

1. They develop a new world view. This new cosmology suggests that African American men receive a new agenda which is kingdom oriented as opposed to self-focused and through male mentoring. African American men reflect a commitment to personal holiness (in private and public), the Great Commission, and family life.

2. New Life Values--African American men must avoid greed and the misappropriation of money. Philippians 4:11-13 gives a balanced approach to life, possessions and conditions. Lane notes that according to 1 Timothy 6:11 disciples are to "flee" the love of money. A Christian resocialization teaches a balanced approach to material things. God gives us things to enjoy, but not to trust (1 Tim 6:9-10).

3. Predictability--Lane sees this aspect as an aspect of integrity. Despite popular media stereotypes, which suggest that African American men are deficient in the area of integrity, African American men must give themselves to faith, love, peace, and the company of spiritual people (1 Tim 4:12; 2 Tim 2:22).

4. Strong Relationships--The keys to strong relationships for Lane are the presence of the servant's heart, a refusal to be quarrelsome, learning to be kind to everybody, patience when wronged, and a willingness to correct those who oppose you with a spirit of gentleness.

5. Intimacy--Lane asserts that the African American man with a renewed mind must reconsider his attitude towards sex and sexuality. He further states that intimacy is not the act of sex, rather it involves attitude, atmosphere, time, comfort and other sensory stimuli. The point of emphasis is that spiritual renewal impacts and enriches not only the public external dimension of a man's life, it reaches into the deep personal dimensions of life so that even his private sexual attitude and performance is changed for the better.

6. New Life Motivation--As a result of Christian reorientation and the motivation which comes

from a positive and clear mental image of what it is one is to do, African American men are able to think and do that which contributes to the good of others (Phil 4:8, 9)

7. Clear Life Mission--the absence of biblical mission in the lives of African American men is rooted in the inability of African American men to comprehend and attain God's vision for their lives. African American churches must be clear about God's vision for men as disciples and assist men in discovering where they fit in God's economy. This would require that the church also be on a mission.[285]

Ministry of Accountability

According to Forrest Craver, the fundamental problem with men in this culture is isolation.[286] This isolation is in some part both cause and effect in the spiritual nurture and discipleship of African American men. Isolation has men caused to be spiritually and emotionally bankrupt and congregations must dramatically change their ministries to men if this problem is to change.[287] This change in approach and ministry paradigm must emphasize "community" relationships with the purpose of establishing accountability amongst the brothers in the community of faith.

Among young men who are serious about their

personal commitment to Christ, there is a desire to have someone who is trusted and trustworthy to "look after you." Among the men at the Galilee Baptist Church who range in age from 19 to 40, there has resulted a genuine closeness which derives from the idea of each man being accountable for their lifestyle, whereabouts, giving and support of the ministry.[288]

> "The idea of covenant in the Old Testament gives to the contemporary culture its byproduct of stability."

Accountability is not only for those positive aspects of one's life, rather these men are committed to the "No More Excuses" ideology of Tony Evans.[289] When certain men have not lived up to their responsibilities, brothers go to them in love and attempt to restore or challenge them to live up to their high and holy calling in Christ Jesus. This ministry is rooted in Galatians 6:1, "Brethen, if a man be overtaken in a fault, ye which are spiritual, restore such an one in the spirit of meekness;

considering thyself, lest thou also be tempted."

When one examines the biblical grounding of the word and its implications for discipleship, it is to be noted that the Old Testament word which closest models accountability is the word "covenant." The idea of covenant in the Old Testament gives to the contemporary culture its byproduct of stability. This stability comes from the understanding that each individual will have to give an account for their life before God (1 Pet 4:5; Rom 14:12). Indeed scripture affirms that each person will have to give an account for every idle word (Matt 12:36).

Covenant is defined as an agreement between two or more parties outlining mutual rights and responsibilities.[290] Covenants were a common occurrence in the Near Eastern culture. Covenants assisted various people groups in encouraging cooperation between different tribes or nations. These covenants were binding agreements.[291] An integral feature of these covenants was the ritual of killing an animal and the repeating of the oath, "this [referring to the cutting up of the animal] do to me and more, if I break my word to you" (Gen 15:9-21; cf. Jeremiah 34:18-20)."

In Hebrew the word for covenant is *be'rit*, which means an agreement or an arrangement. It is derived from the Hebrew word *ba'ra* "to eat bread with," which is to suggest that the contracting parties symbolized their bond by having a covenant meal at the conclusion of the formal agreement.[292] This is an excellent metaphor for persons in accountable and responsible relationship with each other and God. Persons may have communion and fellowship based on the mutual covenant each has made with God.

The Old Testament has several different models of covenants: God and Noah (Gen 9:8-17); God and Abram (Gen 15:17); Israelites (Exodus 19-24);

David and Jonathan, Saul's son (1 Sam 18:3, 4; 22:8); King Solomon and the Shemi (1 Kings 2:42-46); Jehoiada, the high priest and the royal guard (2 Kings 11:4); David and Abner (2 Sam 3:12-21).[293] These "agreements," "leagues," or covenants could be made between superior and inferior, God and humanity, or persons of equal strength. Covenants usually consist of seven aspects: (1) the preamble, (2) historical prologue describing the previous relations (between God and Israel); (3) stipulations; (4) list of witnesses; (5) sanctions--curses or blessings; (6) provision for the deposit of the covenant document and its periodic reading; (7) and the oath.[294]

In the New Testament, one sees that Jesus interprets the Old Testament "covenant" in the new light of His sacrifice which brings forgiveness through His blood shed on the cross and symbolized by the observation of communion and the wine of the communion (Matt 26:28).[295] Paul makes a distinction between the Old and New covenants by focusing more on the saving work of Christ in the transformed hearts of humanity (2 Corinthians 3:16), as opposed to the sacrifice of the Christ.[296] Although Paul sees the sacrifice of Jesus as important, Paul concentrates on the distinction between the two covenants by reasoning that the new covenant in Christ issues freedom and grants believers a glimpse of the divine majesty and glory.[297] Paul sees a difference between the covenant of law and the covenant of grace.

> "Covenant requires those who belong to God to practice personal responsibility and accountability.."

Covenant is helpful here because it reveals that although one can come to the "table" and share in the benefits of Christ's sacrifice, one is still accountable for honoring their commitment to be God's own special people. Covenant requires those who belong to God to practice personal responsibility and accountability which enables them to "stay in the land" by keeping God's commandments. Accountability suggests that humanity is responsible to God and must give an account for all that God has graciously bestowed to us through time, talent, treasure, temple, speech, attitude and lifestyle (Matt 12:36; 25:14-30; Luke19:11-27; 2 Corinthians 5:10). Romans 14:10 advises that one is to also consider the weaker brother; 1 Corinthians 6:12; 10:23 advises that disciples are to keep their own body and passions under control, and Romans 13:1-7 declares that the disciple is to also respect civil rulers.

> "God expects His community to be faithful to His teachings. We are to police ourselves."

One may note that there is both a private and public dimension of accountability. Howard Hendricks has stated that small group ministries provide excellent settings for accountability.[298] Hendricks is highlighting the importance of community by further suggesting that a man who is not in a group with other men is an accident waiting to happen.[299]

God intended the covenant between Himself and his people to help them live by the lifestyle and hold to the beliefs which God had given the church. God expects His community to be faithful to His teachings. We are to police ourselves.[300]

David Schroeder provides five types of accountability structures which may assist men in growing into Christian maturity and holiness: (1) mentor accountability; (2) group accountability; (3) double-date accountability; (4) spousal accountability; (5) one-on-one accountability.[301] Another area that must be examined is whether or not men feel they have a relationship which is secure enough for the trust

> "Men tend to shy away from any unnecessary disclosure of information."

necessary to submit to another's spiritual assistance. No individual would share private and sensitive concerns with someone who is untested or untrustworthy. Men tend to shy away from any unnecessary disclosure of information. This would be true to an even greater extent if they feel threatened or that the person to whom they speak is not one in whom they want to confide. If men feel that they are in trusting relationships with other men, Keith Drury has suggested seventy-five questions which may be utilized in establishing accountability:

75 Specific Accountability Questions.

1. Have you had daily time alone with God since we last met?
2. How many days alone with God have you taken?
3. Have your thoughts been pure and free from lust?
4. Have you dated your spouse every week?
5. Have you taken a day off each week?
6. Have you had a daily debriefing time with your spouse?
7. Is there anyone against whom you are holding a grudge?

8. Is there any emotional attachment with someone of the opposite sex which could develop dangerously?
9. With whom could such an attachment develop in the future?
10. Have you given unselfishly to your mate's needs?
11. Are there any unresolved conflicts with your mate?
12. How often have you had family altar since we last met?
13. How often have you shared your faith? When? What happened?
14. How much time have you spent with your children? Doing what?
16. Have you spread falsehoods about another--slander?
17. Have you spoken hurtful truth about another--gossip?
18. Do you have any unmade restitutions?
19. Are you discipling your child? Mate? How? When?
20. Is your practice of journaling up to date?
21. How much have you fasted since we last met?
22. Have you had nightly prayers with your spouse?
23. Report on your memorizing and meditating on scripture.
24. How are you improving in your relationship with your mate?
25. Is there a brother you should try to restore from sin?
26. When did you last give a thoughtful gift to your mate?

27. In what ways have you been tempted to be proud?
28. How have you given to the needy since we last met?
29. How much time have you wasted watching TV?
30. What about questionable movies, magazines, or videos?
31. Are you completely out of installment debt?
32. How are you avoiding materialism?
33. Have you exaggerated or lied since we last met?
34. Have you been able to ignore carnal, complaining, petty people?
35. What spiritual growth books have you read since we met?
36. Of what are you afraid? How will you defy this fear?
37. How have you played "Team Ball" with others since we last met?
38. Have you had a critical spirit since we last met?
39. In what special ways have you shown love to your mate?
40. Have you been fully submissive to authority?
41. Who is it that you are tempted to envy, or be jealous of?
42. Is there any believer with whom you are out of harmony?
43. Who are you discipling and mentoring? How?
44. Was there a time when your love for God was hotter?
45. How have you attempted to make peace between others?
46. Have you taken anything not belonging to you, large or small?

47. What sexual sin have you been most tempted to commit?
48. Have you a practice which may be a stumbling block to others?
49. Have you avoided outbursts of anger or rage?
50. About what have you been inclined to boast?
51. Have you been tempted to give up? How? Why?
52. How have you clarified your life's mission since we last met?
53. Have you avoided fighting, quarreling, dissension, and factions?
54. How have you shown enduring patience since we last met?
55. Have you avoided obscenity, foolish talk, and course jokes?
56. In what ways have you been tempted to greed?
57. Have you selfish ambition? How pure is your desire to achieve?
58. Is there hate, malice, or ill will in your heart for anyone?
59. Is there any sin, inward or outward, which has dominion over you so that you are habitually falling in error?
60. How have you expressed thanksgiving to God and others?
61. How have you shown submission and respect to your husband?
62. How have you shown love and tenderness to your wife?
63. Have you frivolously wasted words since we last met?
64. Have you participated in fruitless arguments?
65. Do you have a teachable spirit?
66. Have you shown favoritism toward the rich or powerful? How?

67. In what way have you launched out in faith since we last met?
68. Have you abused your power over others? How?
69. Have you deceitfully manipulated people for your own benefit?
70. Have you been guilty of worry, anxiety, or distrust of God?
71. In what ways have you shown brotherly kindness?
72. Is there any sin of another which you have come to tolerate?
73. How have you sought opportunities to serve, listen, and help?
74. How have you cared for the needy since we last met?
75. To whom did you show Christ's love since we last met? How?[302]

Ministry of Fellowship

Patrick Morley, in "Reaching the Disconnected Male," notes that a man is a hard thing to reach.[303] He advises that the natural difficulty one faces in attempting to reach men is worth the struggle. When one man turns to Jesus Christ, it breaks a chain of bondage to sin and broken relationships. One changed man can set a family for many generations on a new course of joy, peace, and reconciliation.[304]

Acts 2:42 states "and they continued steadfastly in the apostles' doctrine and fellowship, in breaking of bread, and in prayers." This example of community from the early church's activity gives the final aspect of discipline African American men, the ministry of fellowship. Although this idea of fellowship is a "common" trait in church life, one would suggest that because of societal and cultural trends,[305] post modernisms and individualistic ideology, the spiritual importance of biblical fellowship has been compromised if not lost all together.

Copeland lifts six questions, which help to evaluate the kind of fellowship and the strength of fellowship within one's congregation.

1. How do we relate at one another when we assemble for worship?
2. How do we interact with each other away from our assemblies?
3. Where are one's group loyalties?
4. What are one's willingness to support each other in time of need?
5. What is the amount of time we spend in the company of others in the church?
6. How well do those who sit by each other during the assembly Sunday after Sunday really know each other?

These questions force the church to reconsider

the quality of their fellowship and whether or not the church majors in "self-centeredness."

To avoid this "self-centered" paradigm of fellowship, one must first define what is meant by biblical fellowship. The New Testament carries several families of words, which denote the general idea of "fellowship." William Barclay, in his volume entitled A New Testament Wordbook, provides an engaging discussion of the various meanings of *koinōnia, koinenein*, and *koinōnos*. In classical Greek, *koinōnia* means an association or partnership. Plato uses the phrase the *koinōnia* of women with men for "co-education." In later Greek, *koinōnia* is used as the opposite and contrast to *pleonexia*, which is the grasping spirit which is out for itself.[306] The later translation would be a contrast of *pleonexia* – the spirit of

> "These questions force the church to reconsider the quality of their fellowship and whether or not the church majors in "self-centeredness."

selfish getting as opposed to *koinōmia* a spirit of liberal sharing.

Barclay continues defining *koinōnia* in contemporary colloquial Greek. Here, *koinōnia* has three distinctive definitions. First, it means very commonly a "business partnership."[307] Second, the idea of marriage.[308] Two people enter into the idea of marriage in order to have *koinōnia* of life, that is to say, to live together a life in which everything is shared.[309] Lastly, it is used of a man's "relationship with God."[310] Barclay refers to Epictetus who speaks of religion as "aiming to have *koinōnia* with Zeus.[311]

In secular terms, *koinōnia* is utilized to express a close and intimate relationship into which people enter.[312] Barclay advises that in the New Testament there are some eighteen usages.[313] Let us now give attention to how this fellowship should epitomize the Christian disciple.

Barclay has seven characterizations of the *koinōnia*

between disciples.

1. *Koinōnia* denotes "a sharing of friendship" and an abiding in the company of others (Acts 2:42; 2 Corinthians 6:14). This friendship is based on common Christian knowledge (1 John 1:3) and only those who are friends with Christ can be friends with each other.
2. *Koinōnia* denotes a "practical sharing" with those less fortunate. Note here that Paul utilizes this word three times in connection with the offering he received from the churches for the poor saints at Jerusalem (Rom 15:26; 2 Corinthians 8:4; 9:13; Hebrews 13:16). Fellowship in Christ *is* a practical matter.
3. *Koinōnia* references the "partnership in the work of Christ" (Phil 1:5).
4. *Koinōnia* also takes place "in the faith." This is important because one realizes that he is not and never can be an isolated island unto himself; he is one of a believing company (Ephesians 3:9).
5. *Koinōnia* also takes place "in the faith" (2 Corinthians 13:14; Phil 2:1). The disciple should endeavor to live in the presence, the company, the help, and the guidance of the Spirit.
6. *Koinōnia* reveals our "fellowship with the Christ," the Son of God (1 Corinthians 1:9). This fellowship is noted in the sacrament (1 Corinthians 10:16). In the sacrament above all disciples find Christ and each other. Furthermore, that fellowship with Christ is fellowship with His sufferings (Phil 3:10). When the disciple suffers he has, amidst the pain, the joy of knowing that he is sharing things with Christ.
7. *Koinōnia* delineates the disciples' fellowship

"with God" (1 John 1:3). This *koinōnia* is rooted in ethics and is not a possibility for those who walk in darkness (1 John 16).[314]

The verb *koinōnein* in classical Greek means "to have a share in a thing." The word is used for persons who have a share in a thing. The word is used for persons who have "business dealings," "sharing an opinion" with someone, or having an agreement with someone.[315] Unlike classical Greek, contemporary Greek of the papyri has three meanings (1) to share "in an action" with someone, (2) to share in "a common possession," and (3) sharing of "life."[316] These meanings are again vastly important to the theology of the New Testament. According to Hebrews 2:14, all persons share in human nature. Barclay holds that there is a community amongst persons simply because they are persons.[317]

Second, *koinōnia* carries the idea of the sharing of material possessions and, of the eight times it is used in the New Testament, four deal with this practical teaching.

No disciple should want to have too much while others have too little (Rom 12:13; 15:27; Gal 6:6).

Third, *koinōnia* denotes a sharing in "an action" (1 Tim 5:22). Disciples are partners with each other and with God.

Lastly, *koinōni*s is used of one sharing an experience or of one who suffers for his faith (1 Pet 4:13). In this very suffering disciples experience the Christ.[318]

The final word denoting fellowship is the noun *koinōnia* for classical Greek, it refers to a companion, a partner, or a joint-owner. In the papyri it has come to be used as a business partner. In contemporary Greek it is almost always a *business* word.[319]

In the New Testament, it is utilized ten times. The first usage is of a sharer "in an action or course of action (Matt 23:30; 1 Corinthians 10:18, 20). Second, it denotes "a partner" (Luke 5:10; 2 Corinthians 8:23; Philemon 17). Third, *koinōnia* can refer to a sharer in "an experience" (2 Corinthians 1:7; Hebrews 10:33). The idea is that nothing happens to us alone. Lastly, *koinōnia* is used to humanity's sharing in the divine nature (2 Peter 1:4).[320]

Frazee suggests that persons were created for community and fellowship and advises that "we were designed by God physically, emotionally, and spiritually to require community for our health."[321] What happens in biblical fellowship (community)? Frazee offers a covenant which provides the seven functions of biblical community.

> **Spiritual Formation**
> In this area, disciples assess their own development in Christ, confess their areas of struggle to one another and set personal goals for their growth in Christ in the next year. Disciples continue to share their progress and encourage one another regularly in the pursuit of Christ likeness.
>
> **Evangelism**
> Each disciple commits to pray for at least three neighborhood households that need the gospel. Disciples are held accountable to pray monthly for these households, their own personal needs and to reach out to homes which have not received the gospel. Disciples aim to win one

household to Christ per year.

Reproduction
The disciples' community is receptive to new disciples, continuing to gain new leaders and seeking to reproduce during the year.

Volunteerism
Disciples commit themselves to support the "Kingdom Agenda" through involvement in service opportunities (youth, children, worship, ushers, and greeters.)

International Missions
Disciples share in world evangelization and missions through prayer, hands-on involvement, greater awareness, and financial contributions.

Care
The foundation of one's community and fellowship is the commitment among disciples to comfort for one another. This care is shown in practical ways (hospital visits, home visits, meal preparation, financial assistance, and prayer.

Extending Compassion
Disciples seek to be a witness in the area of social needs by participating in "compassion projects" throughout the year.[322]

It is to be noted that not every person can do all of these, but all disciples can do some of these. This type of incarnational fellowship establishes that one's church or group has an "approachable personality."[323] Those persons (men), who come into contact with the church, feel at ease and comfortable around or in the fellowship. Second, this type of "service" fellowship engenders the opportunity for others to see that men are not afraid to be transparent in their Christian lifestyle.[324] Fellowship that is biblical and genuine provides an excellent setting for men to see and touch that which is counter cultural and not "self-centered" as evidenced in the apostles' doctrine.

> "Fellowship that is biblical and genuine provides an excellent setting for men to see and touch that which is counter cultural and not 'self-centered'"

        1 Corinthians 12:26   disciples are to care about one another
        Galatians 5:13   disciples are to serve one another in love
        Colossians 3:16   disciples are to teach and admonish one another
        James 5:16   disciples are to pray for one another
        James 5:19-20   disciples are to restore one another
        1 Peter 4:9   disciples are to be hospitable to one another[325]

Each of these principles if properly utilized will reflect Christ's character and concern for the members of the fellowship and also for those not yet a part of the community of faith. The church's faith must be shown through the pragmatism of fellowship and if this is done, God will be gloried and the saints edified.

CHAPTER 4

CONCLUSION

Acts 11:26 reveals that "the disciples were first called Christians at Antioch." Yet, one must remember that the scriptures talk much more about disciples than Christians.[326]

In the first century Antioch, being identified as a Christian meant that one had been labeled as one who had "believed and turned to the Lord" (Acts 11:21) and who had determined "to remain true to the Lord with all one's heart" (Acts 11:23).[327]

Much has changed from the first century until the present. The word disciple has lost much of its appeal to the church culture of today and Briscoe notes that in an era when "laissez-faire" not only can be applied to economics and sexual behavior, but also to a Christianity committed more to feeling good than doing good, and to enjoying rather than enduring, disciple sounds suspiciously like discipline.[328]

A disciple is one who is developing a personal, lifelong, obedient relationship with Jesus Christ in which He transforms their character into Christ likeness; changes their values (agenda) into kingdom values (agenda) and involves them in His mission in the home, the church, and the world.[329]

> "A disciple is one who is developing a personal, lifelong, obedient relationship with Jesus Christ.."

The discipleship of African American men requires an aggressive and intentional methodology which takes into consideration the biblical, theological, socio-historical and community concerns which affect the reaching of African American men with the saving gospel of Jesus Christ (Matt 28:18-20).

The goal of discipleship for the church should be to mature and multiply the believers so that each believer can be equipped and empowered to bear fruit in their living and in their witness to the world (John 15:1-8). One of the signs of spiritual maturity is one's relationship with God and others. Matthew 22:37-39 says, "You shall love the Lord your God with all your heart, and with all your soul, and with all you mind. This is the first and greatest commandment. The second is like unto it--you shall love your neighbor as yourself."

> "Discipleship training is an important element in equipping the believers to carry out the commission of the church.."

Another objective of discipleship is assisting persons to fulfill the Great Commission. Discipleship training is an important element in equipping the believers to carry out the commission of the church and this mandate must be taken more seriously within all congregations so that one's preparedness to fulfill the commission is not hindered by one's lack of training.

Discipleship of African American men will be a more rewarding experience when this training takes place within the confines of Christian community and family. The African American church epitomizes this tradition and admonition. From the beginning of the African American church, one notes that extended family and communal values were stressed as a means of transforming the present existential horror of separation and pain. African American men have a need to be reacquainted with the significance of the church and the gospel that she preaches. Inspiration and information can overcome many of the difficulties raised in this paper.

Another important area is the need to literally "see" models of ministry and tangible flesh attempting to live what is preached and taught each Sunday. This "seeing" can be the bridge whereby someone may come to understand the relevance of Christianity to culture. The way of Jesus does not belong to a specific people, but to all people (Matt 28:18-20). The church must not allow generations of men to live below their calling or never to heed their calling.

When men are brought into the family of faith they need immediate training to understand that the way of the world is not the way of Jesus nor His church. As such, men must be challenged to be responsible and accountable in their spiritual walk as evidenced in worship, prayer, family responsibilities, community concerns, and evangelism. All of this should be undertaken in the spirit of love and meekness within the bounds of spiritual fellowship. If the church can slow down to build relationships with men and focus on nurturing and maturing the saints, men will take their rightful place in the home, church, community and the kingdom.

Endnotes

[1] Michael J. Wolf, *The Entertainment Economy: How Mega-Media Forces Are Transforming Our Lives* (New York: Times Books, 1999).

[2] My research interviews and discussions with Mark-X and other members of the Nation of Islam reveal this to be true. Jesus was a good teacher, a good prophet, and revolutionary, but according to Muslim theology (Nation of Islam) Allah is the only "God," and Mohammad is his prophet. See Garry Banks and Eddie Kinley, Jr, *Sharing Christ with Black Muslims: An Introduction to the Orientation of Black Muslims* (Bridgeton, NJ: BKin Light Ministries, 1995).

[3] This phrase "make, mark, and mature" the disciples is not originally my own. This idea comes from Walter Malone, Jr., pastor of the Canaan Baptist Church in Louisville, Kentucky, in our conversation on the meaning of the "Great Commission" Matt 28:19 for the African American Church, December 1995.

[4] Tony Evans, *Guiding Your Family in a Misguided World: How to Prepare Your Kids to Live in a Secular Society* (LaVerne, TN: Focus On The Family, 1991).

[5] Ibid.

[6] Willie Richardson, *Reclaiming The Urban Family: How to Mobilize the Church as a Family Training Center* (Grand Rapids: Zondervan, 1996), 11.

[7] Marsha Foster Boyd, "The African American Church as a Healing Community: Theological and Psychological Dimensions of Pastoral Care," *Journal of Theology United Theological Seminary* 95 (1991): 17-20. See also William Quick, "Will the Church Lose the City?" *Journal of Theology United Theological Seminary* 99 (1995): 47-62.

[8] Ella P. Mitchell and Henry H. Mitchell, "Black Spirituality: The Values in that "ole' Time Religion," *Journal of Interdenominational Theological Center* 12 (1990): 99.

[9] This term is not the post-modern term used to denote general religious or spiritual curiosity, but it is utilized here to refer to those persons who feel the spirit and are moved to be more like Jesus and in doing so fulfill the commands of Christ.

[10] Mitchell and Mitchell, "Black Spirituality."

[11] Daryl Ward, "Ministry in the City: Who Will Stand in the Gap?" *Journal of Theology United Theological Seminary* 99 (1999): 32-34.

[12] Ibid., 33-34. Although I utilized the four major gaps, Ward lists several others such as mental, physical, family well-being, housing (quality and the lack of affordable housing), poor transportation systems and roads in the inner city, air-quality, and grocery stores which either are not existent, selling their products too expensive or certain items sold spoiled.

[13] Ibid., 34.

[14] John Jacobs, "The Need for an Urban Marshall Plan for America," *Journal of Theology United Theological Seminary* 99 (1995): 32.

[15] Charles Elliot, Jr., Pastor, King Solomon Baptist Church, through his church's Benevolence Society, Inc. has a program called "Jesus and a job." Its intent is to assist persons in the community to become gainfully employed by empowering them with the necessary skills needed to obtain viable employment as well as to introduce these persons to Jesus.

[16] This is important because the lack of employment and higher crime rates are naturally linked. See Walter Malone, Jr., *From Holy Power to Holy Profit* (Chicago: African American Images, 1994); Gregory J. Reed, *Economic Empowerment through the Church: A Blueprint for Progressive Community Development* (Grand Rapids: Zondervan 1989; Theodore Walker, *Empower the People: An Ethic of Shared Bread* (Maryknoll, NY: Orbis Books, 1991); Eugene Rivers, "God vs. Gangs," *Newsweek*, June 1, 1998, 20-29; Lloyd Gite, "The New Agenda of the Black Church: Economic Development for Black America," *Black Enterprise*", December 1993, 5. Gite discusses several

positions and congregations which have started or begun economic empowerment ministries in their churches. These congregations seek to provide job skills and entrepreneurial opportunities for those who otherwise would not be given an opportunity. Churches now own KFC's and auto care factories and are using a kind of liberation theology to transform their communities into areas that seek to give God the glory. These community development corporations (CDC) also assist persons with housing and proper stewardship (money management) priorities.

[17] Ward, "Ministry in the City," 33.

[18] Ibid.

[19] Ibid.

[20] Ibid. Ward suggests that one cell in a prison costs approximately $85,000.

[21] Many inner city churches have re-tooled Baptist Young People's Union and Baptist Training Union to Rites of Passage or camps in the summer which focus on excellence, history, heritage, and biblical discipleship.

[22] Ward, "Ministry in the City," 34.

[23] Ibid., 34.

[24] Ibid., 35.

[25] Ibid.

[26] Ibid., 38.

[27] Rom 12:2; 2 Corinthians 5:17.

[28] Daryl Ward, "Ministry in the City," 38-39.

[29] E. Franklin Frazier, *The Negro Church in America* (New York: Schoken Books, 1964). Gayraud S. Wilmore, *Black Religion and Black Radicalism: An Interpretation of the Religious History of Afro-American People* (Maryknoll, NY: Orbis, 1995). The term "invisible

institution" refers to the ante-bellum church of the slaves which although they (slaves) met in secret was a viable and central institution in the lives of the captive African. The church was unseen to the plantation master, but yet existing in the hush harbor.

[30]T. Vaughn Walker, lecture given at Southern Baptist Theological Seminary, January 6, 2001. See Andrew Billingsley, *Climbing Jacob's Ladder. The Enduring Legacy of African American Families* (New York: Simon S. Schuster, 1990). See also Lee N. June, ed., *The Black Family: Past, Present and Future* (Grand Rapids: Zondervan 1991).

[31]Because it was illegal in most southern states to teach the captive African to read and write, much of African theology, experience, and tradition was translated orally. Until the last 150 years or so academics was not a major pursuit in the African American community.

[32]At this point, one cannot point to a resource such as Masterlife, Navigators, or Discipleship Essentials written for or even with urban men in mind. By this I mean, written to address the "how-to" and identity issues of persons in center city locations.

[33]See Henry H. Mitchell, *Black Preaching: The Recovery of a Powerful Art* (Nashville: Abingdon Press, 1990). Mitchell ties the types and styles of black preaching to West Africa, and the cultural idioms which we see in the African American church derive from these as well. Again, there is existing among African American the holistic and communal perspective which is clearly seen in African American worship.

[34]Sterling Stuckey, *Slave Culture: Nationalist Theory and Foundations of Black America* (New York: Oxford Press, 1987), 38.

[35]This is a present reality even 300 years later--if I or another pastor do not show up in our pulpits on any particular worship occasion, there will be those members of our congregations who get up and leave worship because their pastor is not there.

[36]I have been at my present place of ministry for some five years--November 1995. One of the greatest transitions necessary for me to make was to become a father to each man, woman, boy, and girl in

my congregation regardless of age, length of church membership, and salvation experience. As an African American pastor, one does not choose to become the father--he simply is the father, and this relationship grows deeper the longer one stays in a particular location. See. Eric Lincoln and Lawrence H. Mamiya, *The Black Church in the African American Experience* (Durham: Duke University Press, 1994).

[37]Leon L. Troy and Emmanuel L. McCall, Black Church History for The Black Christian Experience, ed. Emmanuel McCall (Nashville: Broadman Press, 1972), 22.

[38]Ibid.

[39]The phrase "help, hope and healing" is my definition and summarization of what it means to preach a liberating and delivering gospel to persons who are oppressed economically, spiritually and *socially*. Black preaching engages the disinherited and disenfranchised by seeking to share with them a holistic gospel. This gospel seeks to minister to the whole person.

[40]Dearing E. King, "Worship in the Black Church" in *The Black Christian Experience,* 40.

[41]Ibid., 38.

[42]Albert J. Raboteau, *Slave Religion: The "Invisible Institution" in the Ante-bellum South* (New York: Oxford University Press, 1978).

[43]Gayraud S. Wilmore has an excellent volume on the subject of the religious history of Afro-American people: see Gayraud S. Wilmore, *Black Religion and Black Radicalism: An Interpretation of the Religious History of Afro-American People* (Maryknoll, NY: Orbis Books, 1995).

[44]Henry H. Mitchell, "Black Preaching" in *The Black Christian Experience*, 47.

[45]Ibid., 55.

[46]Many older persons in the African American church will never throw a Bible away no matter how torn or fallen apart it is. One

never places anything on a Bible in the home of an older saint. This would be to disgrace the Bible and one's self. Older African Americans in the past and many today take great pride in a preacher/pastor who knows and rightly divides the word of truth.

[47] Mitchell, *Black Preaching,* 55-56.

[48] Ibid.

[49] Craig A. Loscalzo, *Preaching Sermon That Connect: Effective Communication through Identification* (Downers Grove: Inter Varsity Press, 1992), 25-33.

[50] Mitchell, *Black Preaching,* 56.

[51] James Evan, *We Have Been Believers: An African American Systematic Theology* (Minneapolis: Augsburg Fortress, 1992), 2, quoted in Cleophus J. LaRue, *The Heart of Black Preaching* (Louisville: Westminster John Knox Press, 2000), 14. Otis Moss, Jr. has suggested that it is true to history then to say that the agonies of racism are the birth pangs of the Black church. Otis Moss, Jr., *Black Church Distinctive* (Nashville: Broadman Press, 1972), 10-11.

[52] Cleophus J. LaRue, *The Heart of Black Preaching* (Louisville: Westminster John Knox Press, 2000), 14. See also James Melvin Washington, *Frustrated Fellowship: The Black Baptist Quest for Social Power* (Macon: Mercer University Press, 1986), IX-XV; John W. Blassingame, *The Slave Community: Plantation Life in the Ante-bellum South* (New York: Oxford University Press, 1979); Eugene Genovese, *Roll, Jordan, Roll: The World the Slaves Made* (New York: Pantheon Books, 1974). Each of these volumes offers different perspectives regarding the harsh damage done to the captive Africans and the culture and religion which derived from this painful atrocity.

[53] LaRue argues that because of the sociocultural context, scripture had to be utilized to address their plight. The Black preacher was "free" to preach and the result was a "freeing" of his people and the giving of hope in hopeless situations. God wants his servants free from anything and everything that would limit their usefulness to Him. To see how this hermeneutic of freedom and discipleship were utilized, see James Weldon Johnson, *God's Trombones: Seven Negro Sermons in Verse* (New York: Penquin Books, 1990).

[54]Mitchell argues this idea in more technical language and cultural idioms; see Mitchell, *Black Preaching,* 57-60.

[55]2 Corinthians 3:17.

[56]King, *Worship in the Black Church*, 39.

[57]Ibid.

[58]Ibid., 40.

[59]The cultural idiom here is "the Lord will make a way somehow."

[60]King, *Worship in the Black Church*, 40-41.

[61]Cleophus J. LaRue gives a list of other "distinctive" which assist the preacher and congregation in celebrating the sermon and the sovereign Lord. Slave preaching and present preaching is strong in biblical content, utilizes creative language, appeals (holistically) to the emotions, ministerial authority--the preacher is respected as God's representative, the emotive/celebrative encounter between the pulpit and the pew, functional, festive, communal, radical and climatic functions of the sermon, oral formulas, metrical patterns, folk narrative methodologies, homiletic musicality, personal piety, experience, social justice, and the demonstrations of God's power (LaRue, *The Heart of Black Preaching*, 9-29).

[62]Robert E. Coleman, *The Master Plan of Discipleship* (Grand Rapids: Spire Publishing, 1998), 10. Coleman states that the Great Commission is not a special calling or gift of the Spirit; it is a command--an obligation incumbent upon the whole community of faith. He feels that the distinction between the clergy and laity is of little importance as it relates to making disciples.

[63]Ibid., 10-11. This question of understanding discipleship is answered according to Coleman when each believer sees the Great Commission as a lifestyle, rather than a possible option.

[64]Jawanza Kunjufu, *Adam, Where Are You? Why Most Black Men Don't Go to Church* (Chicago: AA Images, 1994), 73-113.

[65]Kunjufu lists twenty-one reasons for the lack of male presence in the African American church. I list those of major concern as it relates to the pastoral interviews I have received. However, all twenty-one reasons must be considered as important. Here is the remaining list of reasons African American men do not come to church--men have felt that a certain attire and dress has been necessary to go to church. The next issue was the issue of classism and unemployment. African American men have felt that if they were unemployed, they could not contribute to the church; therefore, they viewed the church as a middle class hypocrisy. Another difficulty of discipleship was classified as sexuality and drugs. Many African American men felt that marriage was not the best option in relationships and that if they needed more than what they were getting at home they should be allowed to get it without having the preacher or church tell them it was living in sin. Homosexuality among the men in church was another concern presented by the men. African American men also listed having a problem with the concept and reality of heaven. Heaven is an unseen place depicted as where persons go after suffering on earth or a place of deferred gratification. African American men want to receive some of their material needs on this side of Jordan and, therefore, heaven can wait. Evangelism was also cited as problematic because African American men felt that Christians only witnessed to middle class persons who were "worthy" of the gospel. African American Muslims, however, seem to specialize in showing their faith with persons of marginal to low income. Peer Pressure or Street Pressure was seen in African American males as fellowship; they do not need the church because they experience unconditional love and support on the streets. They felt that they could be themselves and had no need to dress up. The final difficulty discussed by Kunjufu was the parental double standards. African American men advised that they were forced to attend church and upon reaching manhood they would not go to church.

Kunjufu received his information through research, questionnaires, formal interviews, and a weekend retreat for men. The most helpful aspect of his research is that Kunjufu provides solutions and suggestions for how the church should respond to each of the twenty-one difficulties in discipling and bringing African American men to church and Christ (Kunjufu, *Adam, Where Are You?* 73-113).

[66]Matt 5:13-16.

[67] Kunjufu, *Adam, Where Are You?*, 67.

[68] Ibid.

[69] Ibid.

[70] Acts 4:12. See also 1Tim 2:5, 6--"For there is one God, and one mediator between God and man, the man Christ Jesus; who gave himself a ransom for all, to be testified in due time."

[71] William Harris, "Why Most Black Men Don't Go To Church," *Upscale Magazine*, April/May 1990, 22-23.

[72] Dr. F. Bruce Williams is pastor of one of the fastest growing congregations in Louisville, KY. His lecture was informed by materials and a sermon from Jeremiah Wright, pastor of the Trinity United Church of Christ in Chicago, IL. This lecture was given on September 19, 1998, at Galilee Baptist Church.

[73] Ibid.

[74] Carter G. Woodson, *The Mis-Education of the Negro* (Nashville: Winston-Derek Publishers, Inc., 1990). Woodson is the founder of Negro History Week and is famous for his concern about education. "If you can control a man's thinking, you do not have to worry about his action. When you determine what a man shall think, you do not have to concern yourself about what he will do. If you make a person think he/she is inferior, you do not have to compel him/her to accept an inferior status, and he/she will seek it. If you make a person think he/she justly outcast, you do not have to order that person to the back door, that person will go without being told, and if there is no back door, the very nature of that person will demand one, ibid., iii.

[75] This is an important note because it underscores the point that freedom cannot be exclusively tied to what one possesses, but by whom one is possessed.

[76] Williams, *The New Endangered* Species, 2.

[77] Bill Hull, *The Disciple Making Pastor: The Key to Building Healthy Christians in Today's Church* (Grand Rapids: Baker, 1988), 11.

[78] Ibid.

[79] Ibid., 14.

[80] Ibid.

[81] Ibid., 19.

[82] Ibid.

[83] Ibid., 21-22

[84] Ibid., 27.

[85] Ibid., 31. Hull speaks to this challenge as well.

[86] Ibid.

[87] Hull calls this "the need for churches to take the Great Commission seriously" (ibid., 31).

[88] Matthew 28:18ff: "And Jesus came and spake unto them, saying, All power is given unto me in heaven and in earth". Matthew 28:19a: "Go ye therefore in to all the world and make disciples." This is a commission and mandate to all disciples.

[89] Rom 12:1, 2 must be understood as a necessary Christian distinctive and taken to mean that Luke 6:22, 23 is still applicable to one's present existential situation. The world will hate the one who seeks to be like Jesus.

[90] Hebrews 11 provides a practical, tangible model to show African American men how to live out this faith in the midst of a doubting world; the church has to assist men in retaining their God consciousness and Christ distinctive.

[91] Hebrews 10:35, 36: " Cast not away therefore your confidence, which hath great recompense of reward. For ye have need of patience, that, after ye have done the will of God, ye might receive the promise."

[92]Hebrews 12:1, 2. "Therefore, since we are surrounded by so great a cloud of witnesses, let us also lay aside every weight, and sin which clings so closely, and let us run with perseverance the race that is set before us, looking to Jesus the pioneer and perfecter of our faith, who for the joy that was set before him endured the cross, despising the shame, and is seated at the right hand of the throne of God." Jas 3:13: "Who is a wise man and endued with knowledge among you? let him shew out of a good conversation his works with meekness of wisdom."

[93]I Pet 3:14, 15. "But and if ye suffer for righteousness' sake, happy are ye: and be not afraid of their terror, neither be troubled; But sanctify the Lord God in your hearts: and be ready always to give an answer to every man that asketh you a reason of the hope that is in you with meekness and fear." See also R. Albert Mohler *"You Are Bringing Strange Things to Our Ears: Christian Apologetics for a Postmodern Age,"* The Southern Baptist Journal of Theology 5 (2001): 21. John M. Frame, *Apologetics to the Glory of God* (Phillipsburg, NJ: Reformed Publishing, 1994), 1-3 notes that apologetics is not a sidebar to the Christian enterprise and the biblical commission to make disciples. Frame defines the discipline of apologetics as that which teaches Christians how to give a reason for their hope or the application of Scripture to unbelief. There are three aspects of apologetics for Frame. The first is apologetics as proof--presenting a rational basis for faith or "proving Christianity to be true." He cites John 14:11; 20:24-31; 1 Corinthians 15:1-11 as a biblical basis for this perspective. Second, apologetics as defense--answering objections of unbelief. One is engaged in "defending and confirming the faith." Frame grounds this approach in Phil 1:7; cf. 16. Third, apologetics as offense--attacking the foolishness of unbelieving thought. Ps 14:1; 1 Corinthians 1:18-2:16 are the scriptural references for this third position. Norman Geisler argues that the apologetic approach centers in the fact that the believer desires to defend the truths that Christ is the Son of God and the Bible is the Word of God. Geisler is correct to argue that one must establish that there is a God who can have a Son and who can speak the Word. See Norman L., Geisler *Christian Apologetics* (Grand Rapids: Baker Books, 1999), 9.

[94]Matt 5:13-16: "Ye are the salt of the earth: but if the salt have lost his savour, wherewith shall it be salted? it is thenceforth good for nothing, but to be cast out, and to be trodden under foot of men. Ye are the light of the world. A city that is set on an hill cannot be hid. Neither do men light a candle, and put it under a bushel, but on a

candlestick; and it giveth light unto all that are in the house. Let your light so shine before men, that they may see your good works, and glorify your Father which is in heaven."

[95]Earl Ofari Hutchison, *The Assassination of the Black Male Image* (Los Angeles: Middle Passage Press, 1994). See also Na'Im Akbar, *Chains and Images of Psychological Slavery* (Jersey City, NJ: New Mind Productions, 1984).

[96]Ibid., 8-17.

[97]Ps 8:3-8. " When I consider thy heavens, the work of thy fingers, the moon and the stars, which thou hast ordained; What is man, that thou art mindful of him? and the son of man, that thou visiteth him? For thou hast made him a little lower than the angels, and hast crowned him with glory and honour. Thou madest him to have dominion over the works of thy hands; thou hast put all things under his feet. All sheep and oxen, yea, and the beasts of the field; The fowl of the air, and the fish of the sea, and whatsoever passeth through the paths of the seas." Genesis 1:26-27 notes that humanity is made in the image of God.

[98]Gen 1:26. " And God said, Let us make man in our image, after our likeness: and let them have dominion over the fish of the sea, and over the fowl of the air, and over the cattle, and over all the earth, and over every creeping thing that creepeth upon the earth."

[99]This is to say that one's humanity is God-given and God sculptured. Black liberation theology also holds this tenet of theological anthropology by suggesting that all persons were created in freedom-- God did not create African American men to be animals, chattel property or someone's product, rather as the slaves suggested persons have been created by an omnipotent divine creator for freedom, given a heart to have compassion for liberation, a soul which signified a space for the Spirit to enter and transform, and a mind for systematizing the black--God encounter. See Dwight N. Hopkins, *Shoes That Fit Our Feet: Sources for a Constructive Black Theology* (Maryknoll, NY: Orbis, 1993), 35-38.

[100] Darlene Hannah, *The Black Extended Family: An Appraisal of Its Past, Present and Future Statuses* in *The Black Family: Past, Present, and Future*, ed. Lee N. June (Grand Rapids: Zondervan,

1991), 37.

[101] Ibid., 42.

[102] Ibid. See also Randy Frazee, *The Connecting Church: Beyond Small Groups to Authentic Community* (Grand Rapids: Zondervan, 2001), 186-202.

[103] Ibid., 43.

[104] Ronnie W. Floyd, *The Meaning of a Man: Discovering Your Destiny as a Spiritual Champion* (Nashville: Broadman & Holman Publishers, 1996). Floyd argues that men want to make a difference, but may not know how to do it. Floyd provides a strong and helpful quotation from Bob Buford from his book, *Halftime*. Buford challenges men to change the game plan for their lives from success to significance. See also Anthony Evans, *No More Excuses: Be the Man God Made You to Be* (Wheaton, IL: Crossway Books, 1996).

[105] Willie Richardson, *Reclaiming The Urban Family* (Grand Rapids, Zondervan: 1996), 11.

[106] Carter G. Woodson, *The Mis-Education of the Negro* (Nashville: Winston-Derek Publishers, 1990).

[107] See Marsha Foster Boyd, "The African American Church as a Healing Community: Theological and Psychological Dimensions of Pastoral Care," *United Theological Seminary's Journal of Theology* 95 (1991): 15-31. The idea of help, hope, and healing has evolved out of the crucible of my ministry experience while attempting to make a difference in the lives of oppressed people.

[108] Ibid., 17.

[109] This is an important covenant because Abram in one sense was cursed; in the Old Testament to be without a male child was to be looked upon with reproach. God promises Abram a family out of which all families would be blessed. This is the same paradigm that the African American church must utilize in discipling African American men. Out of one family (church, small group, etc.) all families can be blessed. Gen 12:1-3: "Now the LORD had said unto Abram, Get thee out of thy country, and from thy kindred, and from thy father's house,

unto a land that I will shew thee: And I will make of thee a great nation, and I will bless thee, and make thy name great; and thou shalt be a blessing: And I will bless them that bless thee, and curse him that curseth thee: and in thee shall all families of the earth be blessed."

[110]Ephesians 5:21-33: "Submitting yourselves one to another in the fear of God. Wives, submit yourselves unto your own husbands, as unto the Lord. For the husband is the head of the wife, even as Christ is the head of the church: and he is the saviour of the body. Therefore as the church is subject unto Christ, so let the wives be to their own husbands in everything. Husbands, love your wives, even as Christ also loved the church, and gave himself for it; That he might sanctify and cleanse it with the washing of water by the word, That he might present it to himself a glorious church, not having spot, or wrinkle, or any such thing; but that it should be holy and without blemish. So ought men to love their wives as their own bodies. He that loveth his wife loveth himself. For no man ever yet hated his own flesh; but nourisheth and cherisheth it, even as the Lord the church: For we are members of his body, of his flesh, and of his bones. For this cause shall a man leave his father and mother, and shall be joined unto his wife, and they two shall be one flesh. This is a great mystery: but I speak concerning Christ and the church. Nevertheless let every one of you in particular so love his wife even as himself; and the wife see that she reverence her husband."

[111]This is not to suggest that there are no other outside influences which also impact and affect one's perspectives, but to suggest that the family has been chosen by God to have the initial and the greatest influence.

[112]Jan Chartier and Myron Chartier, *Nurturing Faith in the Family* (Valley Forge: Judson Press, 1986), 17. The authors also note the importance of Deuteronomy 6:4-9 in providing a basic model for nurturing faith in the family intergenerationally.

[113]Harriette Pipes McAdoo, ed., *Black Families* (Beverly Hills: Sage Publications, 1981), 11.

[114]Ibid., 10.

[115]Ibid., 10-11.

[116]Ibid.

[117]Ibid.

[118]These divisions, according to McAdoo, are now evolving into the "Africanist" and the "Empiricist" schools.

[119]Boyd, "African American Churches as Healing Community," 16.

[120]Jualynne Dodson, *"Conceptualizations of Black Families"* in *Black Families,* 25.

[121]In 1965 Daniel P. Moynihan was the Assistant Secretary of the Office of Policy Planning and Research of the United States Department of Labor. It was during his tenure that the Moynihan Report was published.

[122]Dodson, *Conceptualizations of Black Families*, 24.

[123]Ibid., 25.

[124]Ibid.

[125]Ibid., 26.

[126]Ibid. In 1966, Elliot Liebour conducted a study of twenty-four street corner men. He concluded that they had internationalized the American norms for family roles, but that the oppressive conditions of their societal environment prevented them from fulfilling their expectations. Lee Rainwater, in 1968, concluded that metrifocal families were pathological and detrimental to the personality development of black children. Other interesting studies were completed by Jessie Bernard in 1966; Parker and Kliner, in 1966; Duncan and Duncan in 1969, who concluded that matriarchy and female headed households are pathological and undermine any male-female relationship in the family.

[127]Dodson, *Conceptualizations of Black Families,* 27.

[128]David Moynihan, *The Negro Family: The Case for National Action* (Westport, CT: Greenwood Press: 1965, reprint 1981),

introduction.

[129]Ibid.

[130]Ibid.

[131]Ibid.

[132]Ibid., 5-14.

[133]Ibid., 15.

[134]Ibid., 16.

[135]Ibid.

[136]Ibid., 19.

[137]Ibid.

[138]Ibid.

[139]Farai Ehidey, "Endangered Family," *Newsweek*, August 30, 1993, 16-29.

[140]Ibid., 24.

[141]Ibid.

[142]Ibid., 25.

[143]See Andrew Billingsley, *Climbing Jacob's Ladder. The Enduring Legacy of African American Families* (New York: Simon S. Schuster, 1990). See also Lee N. June, ed., *The Black Family: Past, Present and Future* (Grand Rapids: Zondervan 1991).

[144]Dodson, *The Black Extended Family: An Appraisal of Its Past, Present, and Future Statuses,* 27.

[145]Ibid.

[146]Ibid.

[147]Ibid.

[148]Ibid.

[149]Ibid.

[150]W. Hayes and C. H. Mendel, "Extended Kinship in Black and White Families, *Journal of Marriage and the Family* 35 (Fall 1980):51-57 cited in Jualynne Dodson, Conceptualizations of Black Families," 29.

[151] See Marsha Foster Boyd, "The African American Church as a Healing Community: Theological and Psychological Dimensions of Pastoral Care", *United Theological Seminary's Journal of Theology,* 95:15-31, 1991.

[152]Ibid.

[153]Eddie B. Lane, *Reclaiming The Village: The African American Christian Man* (Dallas: Black Family Press, 1997), 27.

[154]Ibid., 20.

[155]Ibid.

[156]Ibid., 21. See Nathan Hare and Julie Hare, *The Endangered Black Family: Coping with the Unisexualization and Coming Extinction of the Black Race* (San Francisco: Black Think Tank, 1986), 151-55. They raise a (socio-historical and theological) question that should be addressed from the standpoint of scripture and theology. Here is a practical discipleship issue among African American men that must be addressed.

[157]Eddie B. Lane gives several criterion for being a strong mentor to African American men. He noted that discipleship of African American men is the surest way to reclaim the African American village and rebuild African American communities.

[158]Lane, *Reclaiming the Village* (Dallas: Black Family Press, 1997), 221-29.

[159]Robert Joseph Taylor and Wallis E. Johnson, Jr., *Family Roles and Family Satisfaction among Black Men in Family Life* in *Black America* (Thousand Oaks, CA: Sage Publications, 1997) 248-261. eds. Robert J. Taylor, James S Jackson, Linda M. Chatters.

[160]Ibid., 251.

[161]Ibid.

[162]Ibid.

[163]Ibid., 252.

[164]Ibid.

[165]Ibid.

[166]Ibid., 253.

[167]Ibid.

[168]Robert E. Coleman, *The Master Plan of Discipleship* (Grand Rapids: Spire Publishing, 1998).

[169]John R. W. Scott, "Make Disciples, Not Converts", in *Christianity Today,* September 1999, 28. This article is a compilation of the comments made during the First International Consultation on Discipleship in England--September 1999.

[170]Ibid.

[171]See Karen Jones Bernstine, ed., *Church and Family Together* (Valley Forge: Judson Press, 1996). This approach targets the goal of equipping each segment of familial relationships, so that the church builds a strong family and the family works to strengthen the community. See also JoAnne M. Martin and Elmer P. Martin, *The Helping Tradition in the Black Family and Community* (Silver Springs, MD: National Association of Social Workers, 1985). The authors argue that there presently exists in the African American community and family a strong tradition of helping or extended family, which is rooted in African heritage. This tradition is a foundational stone in reorganizing and working to develop a Family Ministry which seeks to

equip (help) those who need assistance.

[172] Manuel L. Scott, Sr., "Let the Church Be the Church," lecture presented at Hampton's Minister's Conference, June 1983 (cassette).

[173] Ibid.

[174] Rom 8:1.

[175] Romans 8:29-30.

[176] John 17:21.

[177] Ibid.

[178] Scott, "Let the Church Be the Church," 1983.

[179] Ibid.

[180] Ibid.

[181] Ibid.

[182] Ephesians 5:25, "Husbands, love your wives, even as Christ also loved the church, and gave himself for it."

[183] Rev 22:17, "And the Spirit and the bride say, Come. And let him that heareth say, Come. And let him that is athirst come. And whosoever will, let him take the water of life freely."

[184] Scott, "Let the Church Be the Church," 1983.

[185] Andrew Billingsley, *Mighty Like a River: The Black Church and Social Reform* (New York: Oxford University Press, 1999), 187.

[186] Ibid. The phrase was originally used by Martin Luther King, Jr. and used in the speech of Bernice King in 1993 at the Martin Luther King, Jr. birthday celebration held at the Ebenezer Baptist Church in Atlanta, GA.

[187] Luther E. Smith, Jr., *Intimacy and Mission: Intentional Community as Crucible for Radical Discipleship* (Scottdale, PA: Herald Press, 1994), 12-13.

[188] Ibid., 170-171

[189] Ibid., 67.

[190] Ibid., 66.

[191] Ibid. See Exodus 20:3: "You shall have no other gods before me" and Exon 20:24 "An altar of earth you shall make for me and sacrifice on it your burnt offerings and your peace offerings, your sheep and your oxen; in every place where I cause my name to be remembered I will come to you and bless you."

[192] Ibid.

[193] Ibid., 48.

[195] Smith, *Intimacy and Mission: Intentional Community as Crucible for Radical Discipleship,* 49.

[196] Ibid.

[197] This concept finds its support in a 1941 letter written by Martin English, a Baptist missionary. In this letter, he believed and professed that Jesus' teachings and life require Christians to make radical commitments.

[198] Ibid., 47.

[199] Ibid.

[200] Ibid.

[201] Ibid.

[202] Ibid., 54.

[203] Ibid., 60.

[204]Ibid., 62.

[205]Ibid., 107.

[206]Ibid., 108.

[207]Ibid., 67.

[208]T. Vaughn Walker, "Black Church Strategies for the Twenty-First Century," *The Southern Baptist Journal of Theology*, 1, no. 2 (1997):52

[209]Ibid., 53.

[210]Ibid., 54.

[211]James Cone, *A Black Theology of Liberation,* 2nd ed. (Maryknoll, NY: Orbis, 1986), cited in Walker, "Black Church Strategies for the Twenty-First Century," 55.

[212]Ibid., 57.

[213]Ibid., 58. Walker has other areas listed, but the above mentioned areas appear to be the more urgent ministry needs.

[214]Walker discusses this from the staffing perspective of "small churches." He notes that regardless of size, the African American church seems to reflect a "small church" mentality because the black church is still largely unstaffed or at least very under-staffed. This dilemma also helps to explain the institutional fragility of the very large Sunday morning church built around the personality and preaching of the senior pastor. He goes on to note that many times these churches are too-dependent on the senior pastor. This model of ministry makes it difficult for discipleship to occur because to disciple men it takes considerably more than just a Sunday morning worship. Yet, without facilities and appropriate resources it is difficult to move to a seven-day-a-week church that is built around worship, preaching, music ministry, and Christian education. See Lyle E. Schaller, *Seven Day A Week Church* (Nashville: Abingdon, 1992).

[215]At the Galilee Baptist Church, we have called this pragmatic practice of stewardship: time, talent, treasure, and temple.

God desires for each Christian disciple to be a good "manager" of each of these aspects of their life. See Mal 3:9,10; Rom 12:1-2; 1 Corinthians 4:1,2 for the biblical basis of these emphasis.

[216]Walker, Black Church Strategies for the Twenty-First Century, 58.

[217]Ibid.

[218]Ibid., 59.

[219]Ibid. Not mentioned here is the present concern of stem-cell research and cloning, corporate injustice and violence.

[220]Ibid.

[221]Ibid.

[222]Gary Banks and Eddie Kinley, Jr., *Sharing Christ with Black Muslims,* (Bridgeton, NJ: B Kin Ministries, 1995).

[223]Walker, Black Church Strategies for the Twenty-First Century, 59..

[224]Ibid., 60.

[225]Glenn Stassen, "Incarnating Ethics," *Sojourners* 28/2 (March-April, 1999): 14.

[226]Walker, Black Church Strategies for the Twenty-First Century, 60.

[227]Ibid.

[228]Ibid.

[229]Mack King Carter, *A Quest for Freedom: An African American Odyssey* (Ft. Lauderdale: Four-G Publishers, 1993), 205.

[230]Ibid., 206.

[231]Danny Akin, *The Never Changing Christ for an Ever Changing Culture* in *The Southern Baptist Journal of Theology* 1

(Spring 1997): 32-41, lifts four Christological pillars which help persons to understand the never changing Christ amidst an every-changing culture. He sees Christ as "Logos"--John 1:1-18 Christ as "Servant"--Phil 2:6-11; Christ as "Cosmic Creator"--Col 1:15-20; and Christ as "Climatic Revelation"--Hebrews 1:1-3.

[232] Carter, *A Quest for Freedom: An African American Odyssey*, 208.

[233] Ibid., 210-18.

[234] Ibid., 219.

[235] Ibid.

[236] Matt 5:16. See also 1 Pet 2:12.

[237] John 15:8

[238] Carter, *A Quest for Freedom: An African American Odyssey*, 220.

[239] Ibid.

[240] Andrew Billingsley, *Mighty Like A River,* 187.

[241] Ibid., 188-89. One would stress at this point the necessary importance of men and women working together in appropriate biblical roles and mutual respect.

[242] These challenges were presented to the writer at the Men's Ministry conference at Galilee Baptist Church, August 2000, Louisville, KY.

[243] James Houston, "Make Disciples, Not Just Converts" *Christianity Today*, October 25, 1999, 28. This article is a compilation of the comments made concerning discipleship at the First International Consultation on Discipleship in England, September 1999.

[244] Ibid.

[245] Ibid., 28.

[246]Ibid.

[247]Ibid.

[248]Ibid.

[249]Ibid.

[250]Ibid. See also Robert Coleman, *The Master Plan of Evangelism* (Grand Rapids: Spire, 1998), 9. Coleman notes that this is also the model of Jesus.

[251]Ibid.

[252]Ibid., 29.

[253]Ibid.

[254]Ibid.

[255]Fred Luter, "Goals of An Effective Men's Ministry," Franklin Avenue Baptist Church, New Orleans, lecture outline, June 1999. Pastor Luter is well known in the Southern Baptist Convention for his work in reaching African American men in New Orleans. He was the first African American to preach the annual convention sermon in June 2001. The convention that year in his hometown of New Orleans.

[256]Eddie B. Lane, Reclaiming the Village (Dallas: Black Family Press, 1997), 213.

[257]Ibid.

[258]Ibid.

[259]Ibid., 214.

[260]Ibid.

[261]Ibid.

[262] Lane argues that the whole purpose behind what the Federal Bureau of Investigation did was to destroy King's influence in the African American community.

[263] Lane, 214.

[264] Persons such as James Cone, Dwight Hopkins, J. DeOtis Roberts, Jeremiah Wright, and David Emmanuel Goatley have all been critical of the "white" homiletic used to interpret the gospel message to African American persons. While this may not be true of all white theology, it is true of theology which has a truly exegetical theology of God's word would have no such bias in the favor of White male superiority, historical devaluation of Africa, and the African world. Gayraud Wilmore gives five areas to reverse this negative hermeneutics: (1) freedom from Eurocentric control and domination (academics and secular), (2) positive imaginary of Africa as the land of origin, (3) social justice, (4) creative style and artistry; and (5) unity of the sacred and the secular. Randell C. Bailey and Jacquelyn Grant, eds., *The Recovery of Black Presence: An Interdisciplinary Exploration* (Nashville, 1995, Abingdon Press), 8. See also Cain Hope Felder, *Troubling Biblical Waters: Race, Class, and Family* (Maryknoll, NY: Orbis, 1991).

[265] Lane, *Reclaiming the Village,* 215.

[266] This is an important concern because even in the writer's ministry he has noted that ministers serve those who are in church--this means that if one is not careful, they could run the risk of preaching a feminine gospel of passivity. This is an issue because most congregations are over 60-70 percent women.

[267] Ibid.

[268] Ibid. 216.

[269] Ibid.

[270] Ibid. 219.

[271] Robert Stein, "Baptism and Becoming A Christian in the New Testament," *The Southern Baptist Journal of Theology*, 2 (1998): 6-17.

[272]For an excellent understanding of this idea, see Coleman, *The Master Plan of Discipleship*.

[273]Ibid., 83.

[274]Luter, "Steps To An Empowered Spiritual Life".

[275]Ibid.

[276]Ibid.

[277]Ibid.

[278]Ibid.

[279]This information was received on Tuesday, January 9, 2001 per a phone interview with Dr. Blue.

[280]Ibid. Blue believes that some African American men see other African American men through lenses of psychological hatred resulting from past oppression and mistreatment.

[281]Lane, *Reclaiming the Village*, 68.

[282]Lane notes that some men spend much of their time and mistakes attempting to locate their identity.

[283]Lane, *Reclaiming the Village,* 72. Lane continues his logic here by suggesting the importance of men having female companionship. However, for the purposes of this paper, the writer notes that God's design for resocialization happens within right relationship between men – themselves, men; men to women and men to community and church.

[284]Ibid., 73.

[285]See Bill Hull, The Disciple Making Pastor: The Key to Building Healthy Christians in Today's Churches (Grand Rapids: Baker, 1988, 112-14).

[286] Forrest Craver, "Promise Keepers, Breakfast Eaters and Drum Beaters: Models of Ministries with Men," Chris Coon, *Christian Ministry*, 29/2, 1998, 52.

[287] Ibid.

[288] One of the aspects of the men's ministry is a focus and sharing of issues, struggles, and temptations that men experience. Nothing is off limits and there is a privacy which is agreed on, so that no man has to be concerned with others knowing his private thoughts. After this type of "unholy and Holy," those brothers needing ministry receive it and are encouraged to live for the Christ.

[289] Anthony Evans, *No More Excuses* (Wheaton, IL: Crossway Books, 1996).

[290] Allen C. Myers, *Eerdmans Bible Dictionary,* rev. ed. (Grand Rapids: Wm. Eerdmans Publishing Company, 1987), 240.

[291] Ibid. Some of the better known covenants were the Hittite international treaties between the Hittite ruler Hattusilis and the Egyptian pharaoh Ramses II, and the suzerainty or vassal treaties concluded between the Hittites and the states which thus became their vassals.

[292] Ibid.

[293] Ibid.

[294] Ibid, 241. These seven aspects are found in Josh 24:1-27.

[295] Ibid.

[296] Ibid.

[297] Ibid.

[298] Howard Hendricks, "Accountability," David Schroeder, *Masterworks* (Grand Rapids: Baker Books, 1996) [on-line] accessed 5 November 2001; available at http://www.gospelcom.net; Internet.

[299] Ibid.

[300] Ibid.

[301] Ibid.

[302] Keith Drury, *Money, Sex, and Spiritual Power* (Indianapolis: Wesley Press, 1992), [on-line] accessed 19 June 2001; available at http://www.indwes.edu; Internet.

[303] Patrick Morley, "Reaching the Disconnected Male: How to Move Men on the Fringe into Active, Focused Discipleship," *Leadership* 22 (2001): 76.

[304] Ibid.

[305] Mark Copeland, Our Life Together – A Call To Fellowship, Christian Classics, *Ethereal Library*, August 24, 2001: 2. Copeland gives an excellent break down of the societal trends which have effected "self-centeredness" in western churches. For example, the 1970's were the "Me Decade"--where individualism and technology designed to bring persons together, easily isolates them from one another. See also Randy Frazee, *The Connecting Church: Beyond Small Groups to Authentic Community* (Grand Rapids; Zondervan, 2001). Frazee contends that there are three forces which have destroyed fellowship and the idea of biblical community: Individualism, Consumerism, and Isolation (177-86).

[306] William Barclay, *A New Testament Wordbook* (New York: Harper and Brothers, 1967), 71.

[307] Ibid.

[308] Ibid.

[309] Ibid.

[310] Ibid.

[311] Ibid.

[312] Ibid.

[313]Ibid.

[314]Ibid., 71-72.

[315]Ibid., 73.

[316]Ibid.

[317]Ibid.

[318]Ibid.

[319]Ibid.

[320]Ibid., 74. See also J. H. Thayer's discussion of *koinōnia*. J. H. Thayer, *A Greek-English Lexicon of the New Testament* (revised, Edinburgh: Tend T. Clark, 1951), 351-52. Thayer correctly distinguishes the words *koinōnia*, *koinōnia* in and *koinōnos*. The general usage of *koinōnia* is fellowship, association, community, communion, joint participation, intercourse, intimacy, a collection jointly contributed.

[321]Frazee, *The Connecting Church: Beyond Small Groups to Authentic Community*, 32.

[322]Ibid., 81-86.

[323]Copeland, *Our Life Together: A Call to Fellowship*, 3.

[324]Ibid.

[325]Ibid., 2.

[326]Stuart Briscoe, *Discipleship for Ordinary People* (Wheaton: Harold Shaw publishers, 1988), 5.
[327]Ibid., 8.

[328]Ibid., 10.

[329]Avery T. Willis, Jr. and Kay Moore, *Master Life* (Nashville: Lifeway Press, 1996), 5

BIBLIOGRAPHY

Books

Akbar, Na'Im. *Chains and Images of Psychological Slavery*. Jersey City, NJ: New Mind Productions, 1984.

Bailey, Randell C. and Jacquelyn Grant. *The Recovery of Black Presence: An Interdisciplinary Exploration*. Nashville: Abingdon Press, 1995.

Banks, Gary and Eddie Kinley, Jr. *Sharing Christ with Black Muslims: An Introduction to the Orientation of Black Muslims*. Bridgeton, NJ: BKin Light Ministries, 1995.

Barclay, William. *A New Testament Wordbook*. New York: Harper and Brothers, 1967.

Bernstine, Karen Jones. *Church and Family Together*. Valley Forge: Judson Press, 1996.

Billingsley, Andrew. *Black Families in White America*. Englewood Cliffs, NJ: Prentice Hall, 1968.

_____. *Climbing Jacob's Ladder: The Enduring Legacy of African American Families*. New York: Simon S. Schuster, 1990.

_____. *Mighty Like A River: The Black Church and Social Reform*. New York: Oxford University Press, 1999.

Blassingame, John W. *The Slave Community: Plantation Life in the Ante-bellum South.* New York: Oxford University Press, 1979.

Briscoe, Stuart. *Discipleship for Ordinary People.* Wheaton: Harold Shaw Publishers, 1988.

Carter, Mack King. *A Quest for Freedom: An African American Odyssey.* Ft. Lauderdale: Four-G Publishers, 1993.

Chartier, Jan and Myron Chartier. *Nurturing Faith in the Family.* Valley Forge: Judson Press, 1986.

Coleman, Robert E. *The Master Plan of Discipleship.* Grand Rapids: Spire Publishing, 1998.

Cone, James. *A Black Theology of Liberation.* 2nd ed. Maryknoll, NY: Orbis, 1986.

Dodson, Jualynne. *Conceptualizations of Black Families.* Beverly Hills, CA: Sage Publications, 1981.

Drury, Keith. *Money, Sex, and Spiritual Power.* Indianapolis: Wesley Press, 1992.

Evans, James. *We Have Been Believers: An African American Systematic Theology.* Minneapolis: Augsbery Fortress, 1992.

Evans, Anthony. *Guiding Your Family in a Misguided World: How to Prepare Your Kids to Live in a Secular Society.* Ponoma, CA: Focus On The Family, 1991.

_____. *No More Excuses: Be the Man God Made You To Be*. Wheaton: Crossway Books, 1996.

Floyd, Ronnie W. *The Meaning of a Man: Discovering Your Destiny as a Spiritual Champion*. Nashville: Broadman & Holman Publishers, 1996.

Felder, Cain Hope. *Troubling Biblical Waters: Race, Class, and Family*. Maryknoll, NY: Orbis, 1991.

Frame John M. *Apologetics to the Glory of God*. Phillipsbury: Reformed Publishing, 1994.

Frazee, Randy. *The Connecting Church: Beyond Small Groups To Authentic Community* Grand Rapids: Zondervan, 2001.

Frazier, E. Franklin. *The Negro Church in America*. New York: Schoken Books, 1964.

Geisler, Norman L. *Christian Apologetics*. Grand Rapids: Baker Books, 1999.

Genovese, Eugene. *Roll, Jordan, Roll: The World The Slaves Made*. New York: Pantheon Books, 1974.

Hare, Nathan and Julie *The Endangered Black Family: Coping with the Unisexualization and Coming Extinction of the Black Race*. San Francisco: Black Think Tank, 1986.

Hopkins, Dwight N. *Shoes That Fit Our Feet: Sources For a Constructive Black Theology*. Maryknoll: Orbis, 1993.

Hull, Bill. *The Disciple Making Pastor: The Key to Building Healthy Christians in Today's Church.* Grand Rapids: Baker, 1988.

Hutchison, Earl Ofari. *The Assassination of the Black Male Image.* Los Angeles: Middle Passage Press, 1994.

Johnson, James Weldon. *God's Trombones: Seven Negro Sermons in Verse.* New York: Penquin Books, 1990.

June, Lee N. ed. *The Black Family: Past, Present and Future.* Grand Rapids: Zondervan 1991.

King, Dearing E. *Worship in the Black Church in The Black Christian Experience,* ed. Emmanuel McCall, Nashville: Broadman Press, 1972.

Kunjufu, Jawanza. *Adam, Where Are You? Why Most Black Men Don't Go To Church.* Chicago: AA Images, 1994.

Lane, Eddie B. *Reclaiming The Village: The African American Christian Man,* Dallas: Black Family Press, 1997.

LaRue, Cleophus J. *The Heart of Black Preaching,* Louisville: Westminster John Knox Press, 2000.

Lincoln, Eric and Lawrence H. Mamiya. *The Black Church in the African American Experience.* Durham: Duke University Press, 1994.

Loscalzo, Craig A. *Preaching Sermon That Connect: Effective Communication Through Identification.* Downers Grove: Inter Varsity Press, 1992.

Malone, Jr., Walter. *From Holy Power to Holy Profit.* Chicago: African American Images, 1994.

Martin, JoAnne M. and Elmer P. Martin. *The Helping Tradition in the Black Family and Community.* Silver Springs: National Association of Social Workers, 1985.

McAdoo, Harriette Pipes. ed. *Black Families.* Beverly Hills: Sage Publications, 1981.

Mitchell, Henry H. *Black Preaching: The Recovery of a Powerful Art.* Nashville: Abington Press, 1990.

Mitchell, Henry H. *Black Preaching in The Black Christian Experience*, ed. Emmanuel McCall, Nashville: Broadman Press, 1972.

Moss, Jr., Otis. *Black Church Distinctive.* Nashville: Broadman Press, 1972, 10-11, ed. Emmanuel M. S. McCall.

Moynihan, David. *The Negro Family: The Case for National Action.* Westport: Greenwood Press, reprint 1981.

Allen C. Myers, *Eerdmans Bible Dictionary,* rev. ed. (Grand Rapids: Wm. Eerdmans Publishing Company, 1987), 240.

Raboteau, Albert J. *Slave Religion: The "Invisible Institution" in the Ante-bellum South.* New York: Oxford University Press, 1978.

Reed, Gregory J. *Economic Empowerment Through the Church: A Blueprint for Progressive Community Development.* Grand Rapids: Zondervan 1989.

Richardson, Willie. *Reclaiming The Urban Family: How to Mobilize the Church as a Family Training Center.* Michigan: Zondervan, 1996.

Schaller, Lyle E. *Seven Day A Week Church.* Nashville: Abingdon, 1992.

Smith, Luther E. Jr. *Intimacy and Mission: Intentional Community as Crucible for Radical Discipleship.* Scottdale: Herald Press, 1994.

Stuckey, Sterling. *Slave Culture: Nationalist Theory and Foundations of Black Americans.* New York: Oxford Press, 1987.

Taylor, Robert Joseph and Wallis E. Johnson, Jr. *Family Roles and Family Satisfaction Among Black Men in Family Life in Black America.* Sage Publications: Thousand Oaks, 1997. 248-261. Robert J. Taylor, James S Jackson, Linda M. Chatters, eds.

Thayer, J. H. *A Greek-English Lexicon of the New Testament.* rev, Edinburgh: Tend T. Clark, 1951.

Troy, Leon L. and Emmanuel L. McCall. *Black Church History in The Black Christian Experience*, Emmanuel McCall, ed. Nashville: Broadman Press, 1972.

Walker, Theodore. *Empower the People: An Ethic of Shared Bread.* Maryknoll: Orbis Books, 1991.

Washington, James Melvin. *Frustrated Fellowship: The Black Baptist Quest for Social Power.* Macon: Mercer University Press, 1986.

Wilmore, Gayraud S. *Black Religion and Black Radicalism: An Interpretation of the Religious History of Afro-American People.* Maryknoll: Orbis, 1995.

Willis, Avery T., and Kay Moore. *Master Life.* Nashville: Lifeway Press, 1996.

Wolf, Michael J. *The Entertainment Economy: How Mega-Media Forces Are Transforming Our Lives.* New York: Times Books, 1999.

Woodson, Carter G. *The Mis-Education of the Negro.* Nashville: Winston-Derek Publishers, Inc., 1990.

Articles

Akin, Danny. *The Never Changing Christ for an Ever Changing Culture.* The Southern Baptist Journal of Theology 1 (1997): 32-41.

Boyd, Marsha Foster. "The African American Church as a Healing Community: Theological and Psychological Dimensions of Pastoral Care," *Journal of Theology United Theological Seminary* 95. (1991):17-20.

Coon, Chris. Promise Keepers, Breakfast Eaters and Drum Beaters: Models of Ministries with Men *Christian Ministry*, 29 (1998): 28-30.

Copeland, Mark. *Our Life Together--A Call To Fellowship*, Christian Classics Ethereal Library, August 24, 2001: 2.

Ehidey, Farai. "Endangered Family" *Newsweek*, 30 August 1993, 16-29.

Gite, Lloyd. "The New Agenda of the Black Church: Economic Development or Black America, *Black Enterprise*" December 1993, 5.

Hannah, Darlene. *The Black Extended Family: An Appraisal of Its Past, Present and Future Statuses in The Black Family: Past, Present, and Future*, ed. Lee N. June, Grand Rapids: Zondervan, 1991.

Hayes W. and C. H. Mendel. "Extended Kinship in Black and White Families," *Journal of Marriage and the Family* 35:51-57 cited in Jualynne Dodson, Conceptualizations of Black Families, in *Black Families* ed. Harriette Pipes McAdoo, 1981.

Hendricks, Howard. "Accountability." *Masterworks* Grand Rapids: Baker Books, 1996) [on-line] accessed 5 November 2001; available at http://www.gospelcom.net; Internet.

Harris, William. "Why Most Black Men Don't Go To Church," *Upscale Magazine* April/May 1990: 22-23.

Houston, John. "Make Disciples, Not Just Converts" *Christianity Today*, September 1999, 28.

Jacobs, John. "The Need for an Urban Marshall Plan for America in *Journal of Theology United Theological Seminary* 99: (1995).

Mitchell, Henry H. and Ella P. Mitchell. "Black Spirituality: The Values in that "ol' Time Religion", *Journal of Interdenominational Theological Center* 12 (1990): 99.

Mohler, R. Albert. *You Are Bringing Strange Things to Our Ears: Christian Apologetics for a Postmodern Age.* The Southern Baptist Journal of Theology 5 (2001): 21.

Morley, Patrick. "Reaching the Disconnected Male: How To Move Men on the Fringe into Active, Focused Discipleship." *Leadership 22* (2001): 76.

Quick, William. "Will the Church Lose the City?" *Journal of Theology United Theological Seminary* 99 (1995): 47-62.

Rivers, Eugene. "God vs. Gangs." *Newsweek*, 1 June 1998, 20-29.

Stassen, Glenn "Incarnating Ethics." *Sojourners 28.* (1999): 14.

Stein, Robert. "Baptism and Becoming A Christian in the New Testament." *The Southern Baptist Journal of Theology* 2 (1998): 6-17.

Walker, T. Vaughn. "Black Church Strategies for the Twenty-First Century." *The Southern Baptist Journal of Theology* 1 (1997): 52.

Ward, Daryl. "Ministry in the City: Who Will Stand in the Gap?" *Journal of Theology United Theological Seminary* 99 (1999): 32-34.

Lectures

Luter, Fred. "Goals of An Effective Men's Ministry," Southern Baptist Convention in New Orleans, June 2001.

_____. "Steps To An Empowered Spiritual Life," outline - October 10, 1995.

Scott, Manuel L. Sr. "Let The Church Be The Church," Hampton's Ministers' Conference, June 1983. cassette.

Walker, T. Vaughn. Southern Baptist Theological Seminary, January 6, 2001.

Williams, F. Bruce. Galilee Baptist Church, Louisville, KY. September 19, 1998.

Interviews

Malone, Walter Jr., Pastor, Canaan Baptist Church (Louisville). Interviewed by author, December 1995, Louisville, KY.

Mark-X and other members of the Nation of Islam.
 Interviewed by author, June 2001, Louisville, KY.

Dr. Eric A. Johnson

Galilee West -3918 West Broadway,
Louisville, KY 40211 – *girteny@yahoo.com*
Galilee East - 3307 E. Indian Trail,
Louisville, KY 40203

Dr. Eric A. Johnson became the pastor of Greater Galilee Church, Louisville, Kentucky in 1995. Under Dr. Johnson's leadership Galilee has grown to the top 25 in Commonwealth of KY in baptisms and in December 2009 Dr. Johnson and the Greater Galilee Church planted a second site at Liberty High School. He is Moderator of the Central District Baptist Association and has previously served as second and first Vice Moderator. He is the Past President of the Louisville City-Wide Revival, and an instructor and lecturer for the National Baptist Convention. He has served as the late night preacher for NBC, USA, Inc. Dr. Johnson's efforts in 2006 consummated a partnership with the Georgetown College for inner city students. He has served preaching professor at Simmons College of KY and adjunct Professor of preaching at Campbellsville University.

Dr. Johnson received a Bachelor of Arts degree in Sociology from the University of North Texas in 1990, Master of Divinity (1995), Master of

Theology (2002) and Doctorate of Philosophy (2005) from The Southern Baptist Theological Seminary. Dr. Johnson is the only African-American in the state of Kentucky that has a Ph.D. in Theology.

He has written articles for both the African-American Pulpit and the African-American Lectionary. He has contributed to several academic and church related writing projects including Oxford Sermons Volume III.

Dr. Johnson is listed in the 1993-1994 edition of Who's Who Among Students In American Colleges and Universities; elected to the National Minority Scholars of America in 1994; served as the 1993-1994 Spiritual Life Chairman of the Southern Seminary Student Government Association; and member of the Alpha Phi Alpha Fraternity. Dr. Johnson is a native of Texas and married to the former Jan L. Wyatt. They have three children.

www.greatergalilee.com